POWER

LANGUAGE

POWER
LANGUAGE

GETTING THE MOST OUT OF YOUR WORDS

JEFFREY McQUAIN

HOUGHTON MIFFLIN COMPANY

BOSTON   NEW YORK

1996

For information about this and other Houghton Mifflin trade
and reference books and multimedia products, visit The
Bookstore at Houghton Mifflin on the World Wide Web at
http://www.hmco.com/trade/.

Library of Congress Cataloging-in-Publication Data

McQuain, Jeffrey, date.
Power language : getting the most out of
your words / Jeffrey McQuain
p.   cm.
Includes index.
ISBN 0-395-71255-6
1. Rhetoric.   2. Language and
languages—Style.   I. Title.
P301.M387   1996
808'.042—dc20   95-48830   CIP

Book design by Anne Chalmers

Printed in the United States of America

BVG 10 9 8 7 6 5 4 3 2 1

TO MY TEACHERS

A word is dead

When it is said,

Some say.

I say it just

Begins to live

That day.

—Emily Dickinson

ACKNOWLEDGMENTS

For examples of power language, this book owes its deepest debt to the writers and speakers whose words grace its pages.

My personal thanks begin with William Safire, the word maven who introduced me to the ways of the word in 1983 and still teaches me about language. I also thank my many *New York Times* colleagues, foremost among them Ann Elise Rubin and Lynn Karpen.

Among the many lexicographers who have made my word study a pleasure are Robert Chapman, the reviser of *Roget's Thesaurus;* Frederick C. Mish of Merriam-Webster; Anne H. Soukhanov, the author of *Word Watch;* and Sol Steinmetz of Random House.

Family and friends deserve far more than simple gratitude. My mother, Genetta McQuain, maintains my word files, and my brother, Dan McQuain, maintains my computer literacy. Extensive thanks also go to Stanley Malless, a poet and teacher at Simpson College; Lynda J. Foro, president of Doing Things for Animals; Dr. Charlotte Fallenius; Steven and Susan Koppe; Robert Feldman of the University of Wisconsin at Oshkosh; Lynn Lawrence and her colleagues at *Unsolved Mysteries;* Mary Tonkinson of the *Shakespeare Quarterly;* David Feldman, author of the *Imponderables* books; and the Reverend Jeanne Klauda and the congregation of North Bethesda United Methodist Church in Maryland.

This book would not have been published without the diligent work of my agent, David Hendin, and astute editing by Liz Kubik, Borgna Brunner, Luise M. Erdmann, and Becky Saikia-Wilson of Houghton Mifflin.

Finally and fondly, I have dedicated this book to my teachers. Limited space permits only a few names: Marguerite Coley of Winston Churchill High School in Potomac, Maryland; Barbara Stout of Montgomery College; Eugene Hammond of the University of Maryland at College Park; and my mentor, Thomas F. Cannon, Jr., of the American University in Washington, D.C.

To these people, who have enriched my life as well as my study of language, belong the merits of this book; its mistakes, however, are my own. Upon finding those mistakes, readers may reach me at P.O. Box 4008, Rockville, Maryland 20850.

CONTENTS

FOREWORD

BY WILLIAM SAFIRE

THE SEARCH FOR power words is not new. Across the centuries, the ancient writer of the Book of Job proclaims the power in language: "How forcible are right words!" In *Power Language,* Jeffrey McQuain captures the force of right words and provides the advantage that can turn weak wording into forceful phrasing.

Language is often at its strongest in provoking laughter. After studying the book *Dawn Ginsbergh's Revenge* by S. J. Perelman, Groucho Marx blurbed, "From the moment I picked up your book until the moment I put it down, I was convulsed with laughter." Groucho added the power putdown: "Someday I hope to read it."

That paragraph uses the alliterative phrase "power putdown," the most recent use of *power* as an attributive noun. First came baseball's "power hitter," followed by the sociologist's "power elite" (a 1956 phrase from C. Wright Mills) and diplomacy's "power broker" (a sixties coinage by the historian Theodore White). Since then, the language has taken "power trips," swallowed "power lunches," and decked itself in "power suits." Madison Avenue now advertises the "Power Popper" for making popcorn as well as a toothbrush with a "Power Tip" for removing kernels from your teeth and a "Power Vac" for sweeping up the crumbs. ("Absolute power corrupts absolutely" is a power saw.) Following the "power boot" of the computer era, the next step in this tribute to an attributive became inevitable: *Power Language.*

Nowadays, with power in everything from tools to ties, it makes sense to add power to language. Too many guides to writing and speaking try the negative approach, telling the word user what not to do. Even Strunk and White, when they took their venerable bead on mistakes in usage and style, began more than a third of their watchwords with "Avoid," "Do not," and "Omit." Many books on English share this "just say no" approach, with forbidding words on words, from "Do not split infinitives" (I like to carefully split mine) to "Never end a sentence with a preposition" (destroyed by Winston Churchill's "This is the sort of pedantry up with which I will not put"). All too often, these negative approaches have stifled rather than stimulated the power of words. A book has been needed to teach and encourage positive approaches to stronger language.

Power Language has a hundred positive things to say about making words work better. I freely assert my prejudices: Homing in on honing terms, this valuable book comes from Jeff Mc-Quain, researcher for the past dozen years of my weekly "On Language" column in the *New York Times*. While surveying modern usage and abusage for that column, Jeff has also tracked historical uses of power language for my political dictionary (from *advance man* to *zoo plane*) and for a collection of the world's greatest speeches (from ancient diatribes to recent inaugurals). The work of a first-rate teacher, this new book adds another facet to his study of English; with fast and funny explanations, he offers an excellent guide to words and wording.

Four steps lead words away from the hesitancy of "meekspeak" (*um* and *well* and *you know*) and toward the self-confidence of power language. Each of those steps reflects a push for power, seeking to replace the longer *(utilizing)* with the stronger *(using)*, the formal *(it is imperative for us)* with the forceful *(we must)*. By following the steps of this powerful companion to Strunk and White's guide, speakers and writers can move from lackluster language to winning words.

The advice is upbeat ("Accentuate the positive"), careful ("Suspect the expected"), and more balanced than mine: "Cite statistics conservatively" but "Correct mistakes liberally." With sources that range from the Bible to the Beatles, McQuain applies apt example to the trouble spots, using errors drawn from actual usage rather than those invented "lesson sentences" that are contrived.

Even with the shortened attention span of the MTV age, powerful wording catches the attention of readers or listeners and adds muscle to the message. (That's a power language sentence; I'm getting the hang of it.) The recommendations of this book include the traditional ("Apply rules of grammar and usage") and the practical ("Break any rule if more power results"). Many of his hundred keys are based on common sense, with "Sound out words" and "Contradict for effect" among them. Especially potent are sections like "Play with cliché"; while most primers on English settle for safe advice like "Omit clichés," this book teaches instead how to work with a cliché, turning the trite into a sound bite. Writers and speakers alike will benefit from these reminders to eschew the fat and make their words lean in the proper direction.

With added energy, words have the ability to amuse or amaze, incite or inspire. A strong word like *power* carries its own energy, while a weakling word like "upcoming" will slow communication and mess with the message. When Bernard Kilgore was chairman of the country's major financial newspaper, he warned his staff away from that powerless participle with a pointed memo: "If I see the word *upcoming* in the *Wall Street Journal* once more, I shall be downcoming on someone who will be outgoing." Keeping the power words and deleting the rest will give anybody the edge in making words count.

Here's what lies in store. In this volume, the opening sections teach how to choose and use words properly. A third section offers strategic advice on how to build with words, strengthening everything from a writer's style to a speaker's delivery. A fourth part reveals helpful secrets for winning with words; the best writers and speakers have long known these secrets for powering their prose, using rhetorical tricks that range from rhyme and rhythm to alliteration and anaphora. Especially useful is the fifth section, covering the controversies of "political correctness" and writing on the Internet.

Read *Power Language* for its straightforward guidance and funny examples. Absorb from it what you need to make your words more memorable. Some of its best food for thought (which, the book informs us, a college student spelled "meataphor") comes in the lists of powerless language at the end of each chapter, including craven counterwords (*nice* and *fine*), humorous and thought-provoking sins of syntax ("At age two, his parents became missionaries"), and weasel words, those measly modifiers decried by Teddy Roosevelt.

This book will lead any writer or speaker toward words that work. Mark Twain, in a 1906 essay on the contemporary author William Dean Howells, took a page from Job on language. "A powerful agent is the right word," Twain wrote. "Whenever we come upon one of those intensely right words in a book or a newspaper, the resulting effect is physical as well as spiritual, and electrically prompt." Take the advice of *Power Language* to heart; apply its words to your words diligently, and experience that power surge.

INTRODUCTION

THE KEYS TO POWER LANGUAGE

POWER LANGUAGE has a lasting effect. Lindy's restaurant in New York, for example, still remembers what Groucho Marx said about his meal there. The waiter, eager to please, asked him, "How did you find the steak, sir?"

"Quite by accident," Groucho replied. "I moved that little piece of tomato, and there it was underneath."

Language is power that everybody can exercise. Knowing when and how to use a word projects confidence, and that confidence grows by practicing with the keys to power language. Using these keys, even the most reluctant writer or shy speaker can overcome the fear of phrasing and learn to make every word count.

Consider the century-old advice of America's greatest humorist. Never at a loss for power language, Mark Twain was often asked for the secret to good writing and speaking. "The difference between the almost right word and the right word," he advised young writers, "is really a large matter — 'tis the difference between the lightning-bug and the lightning."

The finest speakers and writers have long understood that difference. The rest of us must learn to reach for just the right word, combining that choice with others to create what Ralph Waldo Emerson called "the enormous force of a few words." From those few well-chosen words, power language springs.

Power language reveals itself not only in choosing and using better terms but also in building and winning with those words. Too often limited to poetry and eulogies, memorable phrases can also strengthen and uplift the message in everyday wording. Not all speakers may need to be so poignant as Abraham Lincoln at Gettysburg or so eloquent as Martin Luther King, Jr., at the Lincoln Memorial, but the same secrets that have provided power language to poets and orators in the past can enliven the words of a student essay or an office memo today.

Those who grasp these secrets have the advantage, knowing that the exact word will define, explain, persuade, upset, amuse, amaze, or delight, depending on the specific goal of that wording. Their confidence comes from using the right word at the right time, building self-esteem and improving the image they convey to others through the power of words.

Building that self-confidence, however, comes with the effort of applying specific keys to choosing and using words. Essential to that confidence is a comfort with words, an ease that permits playfulness. With increasing comfort in using words, writers and speakers will find that wordplay breaks out in unexpected ways. A brochure for future lawyers speaks of *trying careers,* and a critic refers to the proliferation of talk radio as *air pollution.* The *Washington Post* headlines the story of a car an "Auto Biography"; an advertisement in the mail describes flying lessons as "higher education."

Learning how to make words soar is the point of this word workout. Most language books these days concentrate on how words fail, on the mistakes that sap language of its strength. This book focuses instead on the ways words work, helping the writer or speaker move from sour language to power language. There is no magic or mystery to much of that power, just four short steps available to help anybody succeed with language.

STEP 1

CHOOSE WORDS CAREFULLY

Word choice should lead to choice words, and ENGLISH provides the perfect acronym for the seven qualities of power language: Exact, Necessary, Graceful, Logical, Inspiring, Strong, Honest.

Exact words come from careful choice, and necessary words are the result of limiting those choices. Graceful words allow the user to sidestep cliché, and logical words preserve clarity of thought. The most inspiring words are often verbs, compact and forceful in their action. Strong words are nouns, the backbone of phrases and clauses, leading to honest words that eschew the dishonesty of inflated meanings.

The choice of the individual word should never be an exercise in futility. Weak exercise with words is all too common, from running off at the mouth and twisting facts to stretching the truth and jumping to conclusions. Working out with power language, though, helps ease the frustration of not finding the right word or of settling for a less energetic expression.

STEP 2

USE WORDS INTENTIONALLY

"Think before speaking or writing" is the cardinal rule of power language (and graceful wording leads away from the cliché of *cardinal rule*). The second step requires attention not only to the individual word but also to the ways that words are arranged and combined.

Forceful phrasing comes from exercising words in stronger combination. Studying the proper order of words helps develop visual images for the reader or hearer to understand and enjoy. Problems that blur the word picture, ranging from redundancy to double meanings, must be examined and corrected.

Overcoming the blurred word is a major move toward power language.

STEP 3

BUILD WITH WORDS DELIBERATELY

In a world that communicates electronically, the message is clear: You are what you phone or fax. More and more, communication is reduced to telephone calls and electronic mail. The business world is made up largely of associates or acquaintances who have never met but who converse by phone. A college registrar tells potential students that the written essay in their application makes a difference to their acceptance: "It shows how well you can write, how well you can present yourself." What people say and how they say it become the measure of the men and women.

Building with words for these impersonal audiences requires care and planning. Choosing the right viewpoint — from the personal first person (*I*) to the advisory second person (*you*) or the objective third person (*he/she/they/it*) — is just the start. From power starts to powerful speech, wording follows thinking, and specific keys for the writer and speaker can alleviate the stress of facing a blank page or an expectant audience. Knowing how to ask questions, how to present facts, and how to handle difficult matters of style contributes to building the confidence of the word user.

STEP 4

WIN WITH WORDS PURPOSEFULLY

Winning at wording produces a highly satisfying feeling, appreciated in the past primarily by poets and novelists. The same secrets that enliven their rhymes and fictions, though, can produce more powerful language in anybody's words.

Alliteration and assonance, stress and balance, rhyme and rhythm, all have the power to contribute to the force of language. Easy ways to apply these power secrets can enhance and empower everyday speaking and writing. From oral reports to quarterly reports, winning words make the difference.

Power Language, with a final section on "political correctness" and the Internet, offers encouraging words on wording, but the power does not come automatically. Like any good calisthenics program, working out with words takes time and effort, practice and patience. The rewards that it renders, though, will far outweigh its occasional struggles.

The struggle for word power begins with the thought behind the words. The most common complaint of word users is "I don't know what to write about." Stymied speakers and writers need to move into action, and the advice is endless: Read, talk, play, travel, work, dance, enjoy, study, see. Good writing comes from life, and the more you observe, the better you write. Emily Dickinson rarely traveled beyond her own house, yet she wrote eloquently of the universe she found at home.

Take the first step. Exercise the right words in the right order, and feel the burn of power language. At its most powerful, that burn allows every writer and speaker to capture the force not of the lightning-bug but of the lightning.

Each chapter of *Power Language* presents advice for more power and ends with a list of examples that will improve wording. Note the entries in each list, drawn from actual samples of usage and abusage. (The sources include television and radio, both national and local, as well as magazines, books, and newspapers ranging in size from the *New York Times* to the *Pendleton Times* of Franklin, West Virginia.) As the sentences show, the meaning of a word is not always made clear by the context. When the example contains a problem, it is followed by a power play to make the wording stronger or more memorable.

Some words, however, are beyond redemption; known as counterwords, these terms work against themselves. They may have been strong at one time but have lost their force through overuse and lack of definite meaning. Should these words never be used? Of course not, but the writer or speaker should have a purpose in mind and must understand the risk. Expect counter-words to work against power language, and count on other words for forceful phrasing that will aid communication.

COUNTERWORDS

ALL RIGHT: "All right, that's enough" may mean "just right" or "all wrong."

AWESOME: "Awesome day care" is either awful or awe-inspiring.

FABULOUS: "A fabulous hairstyle" may look good or may date back to Aesop's *Fables.*

FANTASTIC: "That offer is fantastic" can approve or condemn.

FINE: "The job was fine" may describe something done properly or something merely mediocre.

GOOD: "A good amount" is some or enough.

INTERESTING: "Interesting concept" can lead to approval or disapproval.

NEAT: "Neat idea" says nothing.

NICE: "Nice work" may be taken or mistaken for sarcasm.

O.K.: "It's O.K." is easily replaced by more precise words.

PLEASANT: "A pleasant experience" may or may not be pleasing.

SOMETHING: "He's really something" may mean "He's good" or "He's bad."

SWEET: "She seems sweet" may be a sour description.

TERRIFIC: "Terrific look!" is a compliment that may fail to compliment.

WONDERFUL: "That's just wonderful!" no longer promises a sense of wonder; the adjective should be replaced by power language.

I

POWER TOOLS

HOW TO CHOOSE WORDS

1

EXACT WORDS

WORKING OUT WITH WORDS

TIME WAS running out. The television interviewer, hurrying to pose a final question, turned to the Director of Central Intelligence to find out about spying practices since the collapse of the Soviet Union. "It's still fun without the Russians, right?" the broadcaster asked. The CIA leader reflected for a moment. "*Fun*'s not quite the right adjective," he replied slowly, looking for a better word. Finally, he made his choice: "It's *fascinating.*"

A single word can make all the difference. Take any expression and vary the final word to see how the sense changes. Will Rogers, for example, said, "All politics is applesauce"; with only one word changed, that saying turns into Tip O'Neill's motto, "All politics is local." With meaning imbued in every word choice, exact wording becomes all the more urgent.

Nobody, however, is born with the right words. Word choice improves with practice and exercise, producing for the best speakers and writers an essential routine of choosing the words worth using. That routine for exact words, requiring three important keys, forms a word workout able to strengthen and sustain anybody's language choices.

Remember the word *choice.* Every speaker, every writer,

every user of language, chooses the words that he or she wants to use. Poets are especially skillful at choosing rich words, but anybody can use power language to advantage in everyday writing and speaking. Imprecise or weak words detract from the meaning of the message, while the choice of exact words empowers language. Stronger English comes from making stronger choices, and exact wording, when it becomes a habit, can be fun as well as fascinating.

WEIGH WORDS FIRST

"What's the word I'm looking for?" It's the cry of the terminally termless, hesitating to find the perfect word. The searcher stops a thought in progress, retracing the mental steps leading to that impasse, then plunges ahead, too often choosing a word that has little relation to the intended meaning.

During another television interview, a young man was talking about childhood bullies and the ridicule he had received in elementary school. He sought for the desired word and concluded, "I was always being *tantalized.*" That word, however, means "tempted" and falls far short of the two terms that he apparently combined: *taunted* and *victimized.*

Like any good exercise, exact wording takes preparation and practice, requiring some mental effort. Not making the effort, though, may cause bigger problems. A public speaker, reading from notes, had to stop in the middle of a lecture on "the need to help illiteracy" and insert the proper verb for the topic: "the need to *fight* illiteracy." Choosing the wrong word is the fastest way to lose power.

Appreciating the right word is the best preparation for power language. Edgar Allan Poe dismissed the possibility that words cannot be found to express every idea. "I do not believe that any thought, properly so called, is out of the reach of language," he wrote, adding, "I have never had a thought which I could not set down in words." Knowing the word that will fit an intended meaning comes from careful reading and listening, stretching and shaping a vocabulary flexible enough to express any idea. Using that right word at the appropriate time comes with the practice of weighing words first.

MAKE EVERY WORD COUNT

The owner of a health club needed an exact word. She wanted to let a slow-paying member know that she valued his business but that his delinquent dues were causing her considerable trouble and irritation. "I don't want to tell him that I'm *upset*, and I think *angry* sounds too harsh," she said. "What's the right word?" One word worked out best: *exercised*.

In the right context, an exact word can instantly be recognized as power language. It shows its strength, often doubling its energy by suggesting more than a single apt meaning. *Exercised*, with its dual sense of "did calisthenics" and "became annoyed," can be such a word, providing just the right mixture of *worked out* and *worked up*.

Allowing each word to do its work takes confidence. Redundancy and wordiness fall away whenever a single word is permitted to express an idea. When a media-hyped Hollywood couple asked for no more publicity, a columnist for the *Washington Post* responded not with a sentence-long statement but with a single word: "Gladly." Finding the right word for the right position can be as difficult as hiring the right worker for a job, but the rewards come with the proper choice.

Every word choice should count. Power language requires each word to pull its own weight, adding information or developing the word picture in ways that would not happen if the word were left out. The speaker or writer who commands the right words is empowered to outspeak and outwrite those who struggle and strain at the process of choosing language.

Warm up to that process by thinking ahead. What point should be made, and what is the best way to make it? Some people with vast vocabularies seem able to produce the exact word suddenly, as if from nowhere, but most of us need to develop our word lists, learning which words will help and which will hinder communication. Power language requires the words that count.

INSIST ON ACCURACY

A congressman was concerned about the costs of unnecessary medical tests and warned his constituents, "They might take you in there and perform a C-SPAN." The unnecessary testing may include a *CAT scan*, but *C-SPAN* is a cable network. Exact words should be accurate words. Preparation and practice will produce power language, but accuracy is also important, particularly in giving answers.

Sometimes an answer will require specific information. A philosophy professor paused in the middle of discussing the nature of truth and asked his students, "Who was the Greek who carried the lamp and looked for an honest man?" What he wanted was the specific name, and a student in the class responded, "Diogenes." Most times, however, there will be many right answers to "What's the word I'm looking for?"

There are, unfortunately, many wrong answers as well. Winston Churchill had a precise but mouth-filling expression for the loss of exact words: "terminological inexactitude." No matter how convincing an argument or explanation may be, the use of a mistaken phrase or an unclear term can undermine power.

When a furniture company boasts that its products are "delivered faster than the mail," it risks the listener's reflecting about letters lost for years in the postal system. Equally dangerous are words that have long been misused, altering their meanings beyond recognition. *Fulsome,* for instance, does not compliment, and *noisome* is not the same as *noisy.*

"Being notorious," a Hollywood actress confides to a New York newspaper columnist, "it's great for some things. . . . I just wish I was notorious in a much better sense." She may wish, instead of being *notorious,* that she were *famous* or *renowned* in a much better sense. The review of a hit musical makes a similar mistake, listing the *infamous* songs in the show, as if *infamous* were a stronger version of *famous.* Always insist on accuracy, using exact words that make perfect sense.

However any heated argument may start, the same words often echo through the exchange, like the refrain of a chorus in a Greek tragedy: "Those were your exact words!" says the aggrieved party. The opponent responds, "But that's not what I meant."

Arguments often hinge on the precise wording that led to the disagreement, and the quoted person must either back up or back away from those *exact words.*

Most speakers and writers cannot afford the luxury of Humpty Dumpty's approach to exact wording. When questioned by Alice in Wonderland, he insists on the ability to assign meaning. "When I use a word," he tells Alice, "it means just what I choose it to mean — neither more nor less." Too often the audience may take an entirely different sense from the word used, but only the reckless can afford to ignore the audience's reaction.

Using exact words may help avoid the need for an instant replay of language. Whenever a word-by-word account is played back for the speaker, however, there is solace in remembering the words of Representative Pat Schroeder of Colorado, who has had statements come back to haunt her. "May your words be tender and juicy," she said, "for people often serve them back to you!" Keeping track of the exact words of others can be a valuable tactic in winning later disagreements about who said what.

The three keys to exact words — preparation, practice, and accuracy — will produce more power in language, but they are just the opening exercises. Next comes the business of choosing the necessary word out of the many possible synonyms that can answer "What's the word I'm looking for?"

Exact word choice adds to the strength of any speech or writing. The words will echo in the mind of a listener or reader, providing a clear word picture of the meaning intended. In the same way, a single misstep in power language can also reverberate. Four centuries ago, the printers of the Geneva Bible looked for an English word to describe the clothes that Adam and Eve made to cover themselves; the word was chosen, and more than four hundred years later, this version of the Bible is still known by that single word choice as the "Breeches Bible."

The power of exact words comes from using one word to express one specific meaning (or two meanings, if both apply); working against that purpose are *Janus words*, terms that carry opposing meanings. These words are named for Janus, the Roman god of doorways. (His name also produced *January*, the month that falls after the end of one year and at the start of another.) The name of the two-faced Janus has been given to words that offer one sense and also the opposite of that meaning.

Look out below for a list of these double-dealing terms to avoid. Sometimes known as contranyms or antilogies, they are untrustworthy by any name. Janus words make the weakest of power tools; each example is followed by a choice of words better suited to express an exact meaning.

POWER FAILURE: JANUS WORDS

ARGUABLY: "Of all the services and programs offered, public libraries would arguably be among the most popular." The adverb *arguably* can mean "easily argued for" or "easily argued against"; replace it with either *certainly* or *hardly.*

BREATHLESS: "By the time the police arrived, the victim appeared to be breathless." For this adjective, substitute *excited* or *dead.*

CLEAVE: "The note was expected to cleave the couple." The verb *cleave* means "to bring together" (a husband should cleave to his wife) or "to split apart" (the action of a meat cleaver); try *join* or *cut* instead.

CONTROLLING: "Today's topic will be controlling fathers." This word may mean "having control" or "being controlled"; either *overbearing* or *handling* should take its place.

DEBATABLY: "That movie is debatably the best film of the year." This adverb may be for or against; similar to *arguably*, the word may be replaced with *hardly* or *certainly*.

DOMINATING: "Dominating children should not be tolerated." This word may refer to the adults or the children; substitute *strict rule of* for adults and *strict rule by* for children.

ENERVATE: "The entire experience has left me enervated." Originally a verb for "to drain of energy," the word is now reversed in some dictionaries as "to fill with strength"; try *exhaust* in its place or, in the newer sense, *energize*.

MIND: "The student appears to mind every word the teacher says." This verb means either "to care about" and "not to care about"; substitute *respect* or *resent*.

OVERSIGHT: "Oversight of the matter has not helped the problem." As a noun, *oversight* refers to looking over or overlooking; instead, use *overseeing* or *ignoring*.

PASS: "I think I'll pass on the fun." This two-faced verb has a slang sense of "refuse" as well as a standard meaning of "share," and those two senses make good substitutes for *pass*.

PULL: "The executive showed his attitude toward the new product with a single word: *Pull.*" As a verb, *pull* may mean "to remove"; as a noun, *pull* shows an urge to attract. Use either *remove* for the verb or *attraction* for the noun.

SANCTION: "*Sanction* is always the first word out of the government's foreign policy leaders." The verb *sanction* means "to accept or allow"; the noun is a legal blocking or censure. Instead, try the verb *approve* or the noun *restriction*.

TABLE: "The leaders have decided to table that important issue." In British English, the verb *table* means "to put out on the table for discussion"; in American English, "to put away." Replace this two-faced verb with either *propose* or *delay*. (A third face is starting to appear for *table:* "to set up a table for collecting donations or distributing pamphlets.")

2

NECESSARY WORDS

PRECISION TRAINING

SPEAKERS AND WRITERS with powerful vocabularies know the strength of synonyms. P. T. Barnum, the ultimate showman and con artist, was said to have posted a sign in the corridor of his museum to help move the crowds along: "This way to the egress!" Eager viewers raced along the hallway to see this mythic-sounding creature, only to discover too late the true meaning of the word. By the time they realized that *egress* is a synonym for *exit*, they had been hurried through the door and found themselves standing in the street outside the exhibition.

"Never say more than is necessary," warns a character in *The Rivals*. Richard Brinsley Sheridan's comic play, written in 1775, introduced the character of Mrs. Malaprop, whose mangled and imprecise English led to a new word, *malapropism*. Reaching for the verb *obliterate*, she mistakenly comes up with *illiterate*, and her *alligator* turns into "an *allegory* on the banks of the Nile."

Power language requires words that are necessary as well as exact. For any given meaning, though, more than one word may be appropriate, and sometimes many other choices exist. The writer Paul Dickson holds a Guinness record for finding the most synonyms for one meaning; a collector of terms for *drunk-enness*, he is credited with 2,231 synonyms, from *a bit lit* to *zozzled*. Once a meaning lends itself to a choice of synonyms, finding the best word for the context comes from training in precision.

Precise wording, requiring three more keys, produces more power. Whenever a speaker uses the expression *in other words*, chances are that the first choice of words was less than desirable. Taking the time to search for synonyms at the beginning will lead to less backtracking and more force in phrasing.

SEARCH FOR SYNONYMS

The plea for powerful synonyms comes in many forms, but the object is always the same. A secretary writes: "My boss asked me for words to describe something permanent. Do you have any suggestions?"

A strong vocabulary develops through a lifetime of word practice. The best shortcut, though, is a thesaurus. From the Greek word for *treasury*, the thesaurus offers a treasure trove of terms. Similar terms abound for the adjective *permanent*, as any good dictionary or thesaurus will attest. To suggest that something lasts indefinitely, try *lasting* or even *everlasting*. To indicate the ability not to change over time, use *durable* or perhaps *stable*. Other possibilities include *constant* and *invariable*, but the meanings of all these words may change over time; definitions are not permanent.

Finding a list of synonyms is easy but not enough. Each term has its own shadings, which may make all the difference in context. Military reports use the phrase *ceased the offensive*, leading the reader to translate that news of peace into simpler and stronger words: *stopped attacking*. Powerful words provide added strength in communicating; weak words may offer a similar meaning but without the memorable or forceful quality of power language. Regular practice in searching for synonyms allows the writer or speaker to develop an inner ear for words. Listening with that inner ear can help discriminate between a good word and a better word.

Making that necessary judgment adds force to phrases and avoids weak choices. Weigh potential synonyms to find the most potent one. Two other keys, though, provide the guide for determining necessary words that contain the most power.

CHOOSE THE BEST WORD

Hubert Humphrey liked to tell the story of a little boy in a spelling quandary. "I know how to spell *banana*," the little boy says, "but I never know when to stop."

Finding synonyms marks the first step in precision training. The discerning speaker or writer must also know when to stop, learning to choose the best of the many possibilities. A word such as *intelligence* may offer among its synonyms the formal *wisdom* and the informal *smarts;* locating the best word for the context makes the difference. Sometimes a good dictionary of synonyms will help discriminate between more difficult choices.

Cynics suggest that a synonym is often the term chosen to replace a word too difficult to say or spell. The professor in *The Wizard of Oz* stumbles over the pronunciation of *philanthropists* and switches to the easier *good-deed doers*. In many cases, though, the right word is the less formal one, not because it is easier to say and spell but because it conveys the meaning with greater speed and power. From the formal *it is imperative for us* to the forceful *we must,* the user of power language must know the situation and the sense that will be appropriate.

If the word is good, feel free to reuse it. Usage experts warn against *elegant variation,* any attempt to refrain from repeating a word by inserting a formal substitute. *Gold,* for example, becomes *the precious metal,* or a *horse* is transformed into *the magnificent beast.* Be flexible in wording, and try not to repeat a term too often, but when a substitute is necessary, look to the power in pronouns such as *it* or *that* instead of a formal synonym.

Amid everyday words, a formal word may occasionally stand out for effect. The noun *dishonesty,* for example, may be reduced to *lying* if a shorter word is needed; however, the playwright Tennessee Williams underscored the message of *Cat on a Hot Tin Roof* by having his characters repeat the formal charge of *mendacity.* (Note, though, the plain language that surrounds *mendacity;* too many formal words used together may put the audience to sleep.)

"SIMPLIFY, SIMPLIFY"

"Our life is frittered away by detail," Henry David Thoreau wrote, and wording may be equally undone by clutter. Be clear and straightforward in choosing power language. Thoreau's advice in *Walden* back in 1854 — "Simplify, simplify" — proves just as valuable now, when simpler wording is almost always better.

In a television comedy, an exasperated man struggles to understand a series of complicated directions. Finally, he pleads with an official to explain them simply. "Talk to me like I'm four years old," he says, and the official points him easily to his destination.

The goal of using simple words well sounds easy enough, but far too few speakers and writers have achieved it. After the death of a popular lawyer, one of his clients was asked to explain the lawyer's effectiveness for an obituary in the *New York Times.* "He could articulate complex matters in the simplest of terms," the client said, "so that juries and judges were deeply moved." Formal words may impress, but normal words have a better chance to move the reader or listener.

Even the best users of familiar synonyms, though, must control themselves. A recent newspaper article on antismoking policies — "for helping smokers reduce lessen their smoking" — needs editing to cut either *reduce* or *lessen*. Two synonyms are not better than one when used together; either verb works better alone.

Daniel Webster, the early American statesman and a famed orator, was a synonymist without equal, but he could also be an audience's worst nightmare. In addressing Congress, Senator Webster would consider aloud all the possibilities for expressing his meaning: "that these roads, avenues, routes of travel, highways, converge, meet, come together here."

Listeners prefer a single term to that type of vocabulary list. Simplifying the possibilities to offer that single necessary word pushes everyday wording toward power language. Webster, however, could also parody the overly formal style, dismissing one long-winded senator as "a preposterous aggregation of heterogeneous paradoxes and perdurable peremptorences."

In ancient Greece, a physician expressed opinions about handling language that should still be considered advice worth heeding: "The chief virtue that language can have is clearness, and nothing detracts from it so much as the use of unfamiliar words." Emphasizing strong, familiar words will empower any message.

Work with short, familiar words to add force and feeling. Testing for necessary words can frequently uncover useless terms, ones that can be removed without harming the meaning. Delete those words that fail to add meaning to the message, but at the same time be careful not to abridge too far. Executives of a Delaware grocery chain wanted to shorten the job title for the person who manages their refrigerated section of produce and perishable foods. The new title came out with a deadly twist: Perishable Manager.

Choosing necessary words helps avoid needless wording. Any use of useless terms depletes power and detracts from the message. In the following sentences from business communications and newspaper reports, there are misguided modifiers, unneeded nouns, and wordy verbs, all of which may be removed from the sentences without changing their meaning. For precision training, look for the unnecessary word in each quoted sentence. Eliminating these extra words can save the speaker or writer valuable time and space, allowing room for language that powers the message.

EXTRANEOUS EXPRESSIONS

MODIFIERS

"The ongoing battle is raging out of control." (Anything that *is* raging may be considered *ongoing*, an adjective better off going.)

"They insisted that they were attacked by really big animals." (Adverbs may lend emphasis, but the meaningless *really* adds nothing but two syllables.)

"Entrance to the property should be restricted to the said person." (Lawyers love *said* as an adjective, but the word should usually be left unsaid.)

"Firstly, let me begin my explanation by insisting I have done nothing wrong or improper." ("Firstly" should rarely begin a sentence, and it should never start a sentence that contains "let me begin.")

"I am absolutely, positively certain of the innocence of the accused." (Here is a two-for-one; *certain* needs neither *absolutely* nor *positively* to make its case.)

"The fundamental obstacle is basically the lack of funds." (Here is a fundamental rule: *basically* is unnecessary.)

"This year he has seemed unnecessarily depressed by his present circumstances." (The adjective *present* should almost always be absent.)

NOUNS

"We are no longer facing a crisis situation." (Try the same sentence without *situation.*)

"That couple has been going through a breakup phase recently." (*Breakup* is enough; *phase* is filler.)

"Close vicinity to historic area." (This fragment from a travel advertisement adds nothing to the message by using *vicinity.*)

"Pilots complained that the visibility factor was too limited." (Factor out the use of *factor* in officious-sounding sentences.)

"The dishonesty thing seemed to bother the rank-and-file members." (Despite widespread overuse of the noun, *thing* should frequently be deleted.)

"She was anxious about the selection outcome for the new job." (The noun *outcome* is included in any selection and should outgo.)

"The noise from the dance activity disturbed other residents of the neighborhood." (If the dance is loud enough to disturb others, it needs no added *activity.*)

VERBS

"You have got to complete the project by noon Thursday." (The use of *have* is specific enough; *got* adds nothing.)

"The problem is is a lack of resources for the planned construction." (Despite a growing use of the unnecessarily doubled *is* in spoken English, a single *is* is almost always enough.)

"He must will enter the competition before the end of the match." (*Will* should have its own way; *must* can go, or lose *will* if *must* is required.)

"The owners do have enough money to make concessions to

the players." (All that *do* can do is emphasize what *have* already says.)

"Any concerned parent should go stop the situation from developing." (Stop this overuse of *go,* which takes the message nowhere.)

"Another solution might would contribute to the problem." (*Might* suggests possibility, and *would* is stronger, indicating probability; together, the verbs signify nothing.)

"What he had had was a bad cold." (A doubled *had* may make an audience tense; try a single *had* for enough sense of the past.)

3

GRACEFUL WORDS

CLICHÉ STADIUM

THE SENATOR WAS explaining his political views to a nation-wide television audience. The *tragic flaw* in our policy, he said, resulted from a *rosy scenario,* and America's leaders had *laid out a road map,* complete with an *escape valve,* in case of finding our *confidence eroded.*

Words have the power to move or impress, but not when they have been overused. Even powerful people can increase their effectiveness by choosing more potent language. Not every flaw need be *tragic* or *fatal,* and confidence should not always be *eroded.* The overuse of well-worn words, in fact, can erode the audience's confidence in the speaker's message, a dangerous pitfall for any language user.

Pitfall itself is overused, rarely if ever in need of *dangerous* as a modifier. The move toward power language requires the release of tired terms in favor of more energetic expressions. Three keys to graceful words lead away from the trite and toward the right.

SUSPECT THE EXPECTED

Pitfall is a good example of the need to suspect the expected. Originally, a pitfall was a physical trap or snare, specifically, a deep hole covered or hidden with branches and limbs. The unsuspecting quarry, animal or human, was drawn onto the flimsy cover, which would give way and trap the victim.

The noun *pitfall* dates back half a millennium, but its literal meaning long ago gave way to a figurative sense: "hidden problem or danger." Nowadays the word is rarely used for a physical trap. Every trouble, major or minor, can now can be called a *pitfall,* and the overuse has drained the power from the word.

A similarly fallen word is *windfall.* This word, which is widely overused, indicates a sudden gain or unexpected advantage; like *pitfall,* it was far more picturesque in its literal sense. *Windfall,* in its earliest uses, referred to rewards reaped from the wind, when gusts would blow pieces of fruit off a tree for the benefit of gatherers below. That powerful image has been all but lost in the corporate world's *windfall profits.*

A first step in reclaiming the power of words is to visualize the meaning. The minefield of overused words would become less dangerous if every user of *minefield* visualized the explosions that come with any misstep. Uplifting writers who reach for such verbs as *rocket* or *tower* should think first of the literal senses and not stretch their meanings to include minor increases in height.

Visualizing a term allows the user to understand the chosen word and decide on its appropriateness. Even a verb as simple as *uplift* can take on extra power. With a visual sense of its original meaning — "lifting up" — the word provides a powerful image for the user to see and, as a result, find uplifting. Any word choice that comes too easily or works against its literal meaning should be suspect.

SEPARATE WEDDED WORDS

Think of *unmitigated*. Quick — what is the obvious choice for the next word? It is *gall*, of course, and the high probability that the intended phrase will be *unmitigated gall* turns these terms into wedded words. Whenever the next word is abundantly clear (as in the use of *clear* after *abundantly*), wedded words become a problem. The audience needs clear word pictures that catch the imagination, not tired word pairs that lack creative or expressive power.

A college paper comes back with high marks but with a circle around a trite phrase in the first paragraph. The student, trying to convey the lack of conscience displayed by characters in a novel, called them *morally bankrupt*. Again, wedded words have distracted from the freshness of a word picture.

The government, no more aware of the problem, often expresses *cautious optimism*. This phrase, made popular by Ronald Reagan when he was president, has become a staple of political comment. Like *guarded optimism*, however, it has a limiting word used so often with the noun that the qualifier fails to qualify.

To check for overworked expressions, notice that the opposite expression of these wedded words is rarely heard. *Guarded pessimism* or *cautious pessimism* has made no inroads into the language any more than *morally enriched*. On good authority, trust that nobody ever begins a sentence with *I have it on bad authority*. In the same way, *famous last words* is never varied to cover *famous first words*.

The predictability problem runs especially high when words have been paired so often that they lose their meaning. Consider the following adjectives (column A) and nouns (column B) in describing difficulty or uncertainty:

A	B
1. abnormal	a. activity
2. controversial	b. circumstances

3. critical	c. condition
4. delicate	d. conflict
5. desperate	e. issues
6. difficult	f. matter
7. divisive	g. politics
8. intense	h. question
9. pressing	i. situation
10. serious	j. times

Any adjective from column A joins any noun from column B in a highly predictable phrase. These wedded words need separation because frequent pairings have dulled their meaning, undercutting any chance of unexpected language. Stretch for the surprising word whenever the first choice seems dull or monotonous. Vary the choice of words without bending the meaning too far, and the results can be powerful.

PLAY WITH CLICHÉ

Fresh as the month of May is a word picture far past its freshness. In the fourteenth century, the English poet Geoffrey Chaucer used that expression, perhaps even then a cliché, to describe a young squire in *The Canterbury Tales.* Six centuries later, the same simile seems trite and tired, unable to conjure an image of freshness.

Throwing out the cliché is one approach to power language. The ability to spot these tired expressions takes practice, but the rewards are enormous. The ability to remove *cut to the chase* or *bottom line* from business jargon or *fatal flaw* and *cautious optimism* from political comments will set the moving word apart from the mundane.

Once a cliché is recognized, however, an experienced writer or speaker can make a play on it, creating a fresh look at the words. The political columnist William Safire calls a book on language *Quoth the Maven,* using rhyme to rework Edgar Allan Poe's poetic line "Quoth the Raven." Michael Wines of the *New York Times,* writing of the White House's optimistic spin on bad news, notes that the optimism is *more than spin deep,* a play on beauty's being more than *skin deep.* Senator Lloyd Bentsen scored points against Dan Quayle during a debate of vice presidential candidates in 1988 with "you're no Jack Kennedy"; when Governor Bill Clinton of Arkansas became the Democrats' 1992 candidate for president, Ronald Reagan successfully recycled it: "This fellow they've nominated claims he's the new Thomas Jefferson. Well, let me tell you something. I knew Thomas Jefferson. He was a friend of mine. And, Governor, you're no Thomas Jefferson."

Outside politics, recycling works just as well. The country singer Garth Brooks performs a song about having "Friends in Low Places," the reverse of the *high places* that the cliché usually celebrates. The motto of the United Negro College Fund — "A mind is a terrible thing to waste" — has been reworked by dieters: "A waist is a terrible thing to mind." Pet owners appreciate the sentiment of "Don't cry over spilled milk — get a cat," and drivers, mindful that "Two wrongs don't make a right," are now reminded that "Two rights don't make a left." The saying "Live and let live" has been done to death, but the reworked forms have ranged from a motto for an AIDS clinic ("Give and let live") to the title of a James Bond adventure *(Live and Let Die).*

Shaping up a graceless cliché, however, is just the beginning. Power comes with words that will catch the audience's attention. The writer or speaker must move beyond the expected wording to find fresh, unfamiliar ways to paint a word picture.

A witness in a court case is asked to talk about car repairs. Explaining to the judge and jury that he lacks professional status as a repairman, he finds a fresh way to refer to his weekend hobby: "I'm a shade tree mechanic." The image of amateur status comes across in that word picture of a relaxed approach to auto mechanics. Similarly, a young woman tries to warn her friends about a boyfriend she has caught with other women; she worked the evening shift and discovered his infidelity only when she had time off. "He's a night crawler," she says, word-painting the roaming Romeo. A new word picture refreshes; a cliché may leave the message in danger of failing, a condition known in the medical community as *circling the drain*.

Not all clichés, of course, are necessarily wrong; in fact, the majority of them may be trite but true. Old American expressions, such as *paddle your own canoe*, were once recognized as clichés but then dropped out of frequent use. That aging term, which means "make your own way," is sometimes still heard in a longer variant: "Love many, hate few, always paddle your own canoe." In most cases, though, a trite phrase may be replaced by a single word for expressing the information without boring the imagination.

Many communicators adamantly oppose trite terms. The host of a cable television show about money sent out a memo forbidding his staff to use clichés. Not even the language police, however, can stop the overworking of some words.

Sports and business expressions are particularly rife with clichés. Equipment must be *state of the art*, the action must be *dramatic*, and the stakes of games are always *high*, featuring situations that are *sensitive*. Those in business who are put out by *input* and wonder whether computers produce progress in *real time* need to be alert to these tired terms. By the same token (a tired term for *similarly*), copywriters must learn to play with cliché and separate wedded words, especially those as shackled as *ironclad* and *alibi*.

Following are fifty of the clichés most frequently identified by business leaders as weak words. After each entry, either a word or a short phrase is offered to counteract the cliché. Look for the trite term in each sentence, and consider words to replace it. Notice especially the power of single words as substitutes, able to knock wordy phrases out of the ballpark.

TRITE TERMS

"Frankly, I am sick and tired of corporate indifference." (Either *sick* or *tired* will do for *sick and tired.*)

"Their estimate of the final costs missed by a mile." (*Widely differed* or just *missed* is enough for *missed by a mile.*)

"The leaders tried to describe a worst-case scenario for the troops." (*The worst possibility* or even *the worst case* can take the place of the overused *worst-case scenario.*)

"That driver doesn't have a clue about the roads in this area." (Replace *doesn't have a clue* with *is uninformed* or *is ignorant.*)

"Taking control of that company was a piece of cake." (Like *easy as pie,* this metaphor is overused; replace it with *easy* or *simple.*)

"The players were on cloud nine about the team's performance in the playoffs." (*Elated* or *ecstatic* would make a happier choice than *on cloud nine.*)

"The comic's performance at the banquet was completely over the top." (Try *outrageous* or *exaggerated* for *over the top.*)

"Her prospectus should cover the company, its earnings, the whole nine yards." (Shorten *the whole nine yards* to *everything.*)

"They have been biding their time until the merger." (*Waiting patiently* is enough to cover *biding their time.*)

"Ever since his promotion, he has shown his true colors." (Replace any use of *true colors* with *true self* or *reality.*)

"That insurance agent is an out-and-out thief." (Out with the modifier *out-and-out*; use *outright* or *obvious* instead.)

"Those investors have been playing God with the future of this company." (Try *manipulating* or simply *playing with* for the cliché *playing God with.*)

"His last suggestion was from out of left field." (A baseball cliché, *from out of left field* can be replaced with *unexpected* or *strange.*)

"Our next commercial should knock the socks off the audience." (*Surprise* or *impress* should cover *knock the socks off.*)

"That fragrance is out of this world." (Unless *extraterrestrial* is meant, the proper description for *out of this world* should be *delightful.*)

"The bottom line is that their shareholders lost money last year." (Excise *bottom line,* and insert *result* or *effect.*)

"She is our one and only spokesperson." (*Unique* or only *only* should be used, not *one and only.*)

"The board of directors may decide to take the bull by the horns." (Either *take action* or *intervene* will surely convey *take the bull by the horns.*)

"That leaves us to mop it up after the product fails." (*Clean up* or *fix it* is the sense of *mop it up.*)

"Other companies may try to push the envelope in product development." (Simpler terms for *push the envelope* are *innovate* and *experiment.*)

"The remainder of the work week will be business as usual." (In place of *business as usual,* either *normal* or *as expected* means business.)

"That division's problems last quarter should have been our wake-up call." (Notice that *alert* or *notice* is enough for *wake-up call.*)

"One false alarm should not prevent our vigilance in the future." (*Error* or *mistake* would be the right word for *false alarm.*)

"He seems to be a nervous wreck about the deal." (Use *panicky* or *worried* to replace *a nervous wreck.*)

"We're spending time reinventing the wheel here." (A better term for *reinventing the wheel* is *needlessly* or *unnecessarily.*)

"The lower-level managers were advised to get with the program as soon as possible." (Use *adopt the right attitude* or *adapt to the system* for *get with the program.*)

"Other companies have decided to take a crack at the same method." (For *take a crack at*, try either *try* or *attempt*.)

"The officers decided they had been taken for a ride." (The slang *conned* or the standard *tricked* should work better than *taken for a ride*.)

"He decided to go out on a limb with the new proposal." (*Take a risk* or *be daring* fits the meaning of *go out on a limb*.)

"They have reached the point of no return with the old system." (Limit the word choice to *limit* or *boundary* for the saying *point of no return*.)

"Market returns for the next quarter will indicate how well we can weather the storm." (*Endure* or *overcome trouble* is a clear replacement for *weather the storm*.)

"The company banquet was fit for a king." (*Rich* or the elegant *sumptuous* takes over for the royal cliché *fit for a king*.)

"From the get-go, the new project has had its difficulties." (Use *from the start* or *since beginning* for the well-traveled phrase *from the get-go*.)

"She can produce the new data in a New York minute." (Reduce the regionalism *in a New York minute* to *fast* or *quickly*.)

"'We can do better without the Monday morning quarterbacking,' said the chairman." (The football cliché *Monday morning quarterbacking* should be covered by *late advice* or *hindsight*.)

"That interview of the executive proved to be up close and personal." (Either *intimate* or just *personal* should replace *up close and personal*.)

"The perpetrators of this marketing blunder should not be allowed to get off scot-free." (The sense of *get off scot-free* may be expressed as *go unpunished* or *escape blame*.)

"The bank director was caught red-handed in the midst of the embezzlement scheme." (Use *found out* or *discovered* instead of *caught red-handed*.)

"Find out who else is on deck for the new position." (Available replacements for *on deck* include *ready* and *available*.)

"The investors decided to get out of Dodge when the declining prices fell even further." (*Leave* or *depart* expresses the same meaning as this shortened form of the Western lingo *get out of Dodge City*.)

"His bosses go ballistic when he spends more than the budget allows." (*Go ballistic* is a newer version of *hit the roof* and should be changed to *become furious* or *explode*.)

"The company has undergone a sea change from its earlier image." (A Shakespearean invention, *sea change* should be replaced by the simpler *change* or *transformation*.)

"Not very often are his estimates even in the ball park." (Another baseball cliché, *in the ball park* may be expressed as *close* or *reasonable*.)

"Her client told her to cut to the chase." (As a scene-changing cliché from action films, *cut to the chase* is better replaced with *hurry* or *get to the point*.)

"The company asked the government to provide a level playing field to help it compete." (*Equal time* or *fair play* is the same idea as *a level playing field*.)

"'Hold the phone,' the chairman said to the board, 'and consider what you're doing.'" (A shorter, stronger term for *hold the phone* would be *wait* or *pause*.)

"The stockholder was invited to put in her two cents' worth on the prospectus." (In place of *put in her two cents' worth*, either *advise* or *give her view* should be enough.)

"They decided to keep some of the directors out of the loop about the possible reorganization." (As a bureaucratic version of *in the dark*, the phrase *out of the loop* is better expressed as *uninformed* or *unknowing*.)

"This new product should be more than just run of the mill." (Replace *run of the mill* with *average* or *ordinary*.)

"Until the merger is announced, the company will be on pins and needles about the outcome." (Stick to a single word for *pins and needles: anxious* if the company is upset, *eager* if excited.)

4

LOGICAL WORDS

MOVING MODIFIERS

LANGUAGE NEEDS LOGIC. The Greek root of *logic* is *logos*, a term that means both "word" and "reason," but the reasoning behind word choices is not always clear:

- An actor dashes into a Washington convenience store before an audition. When he orders coffee to go, the clerk reaches for the steaming pot, pausing only to ask, "Do you want it in a cup?"
- A New York horse trainer explains that horses refuse to take falls, adding, "It goes against their human nature."
- A Los Angeles judge listens carefully to testimony about a suspicious sound and finally wonders aloud "where that noise was seen."

"Common sense," Voltaire wrote in his philosophical dictionary in 1764, "is not so common," and little appears to have changed in the intervening centuries. Today's speakers and writers would be well advised to consider the need for that common sense, which lies at the heart of words that communicate. Reaching for logical words will produce meaning that reaches the audience without mangling the message.

Be sure to consider a word's age as well as its connotations.

The simple *dressed* may be replaced with the shorter *clad* or *decked,* but only when an older or poetic term is sought. Finding a synonym for the modifier *insistent* is not so easy, though. This neutral adjective may be equated with *determined* or *strong-willed* to compliment a person; calling the same person *stubborn* or *pig-headed,* or even *mulish,* is hardly a compliment. Make the modifier fit the message, or suffer the consequences of comparing somebody to a mule.

MODIFY CLEARLY

"Be clear," Strunk and White advise in *The Elements of Style,* but clarifying difficult wording is not always simple. Everybody has heard the type of sentence that seems to make sense but fails to reach a sensible conclusion. A frazzled announcer says, "I can't go on the radio looking like this," and needs to be reminded that radio announcers remain unseen. Similarly, a witness tries to remember the description of an alleged criminal and comes up with "a light-headed man"; regardless of the man's sense of balance, the correct term for his physical appearance is *light-haired,* not *light-headed.*

Finding the logical modifier helps empower language. An illogical choice may lead to head scratching and confused looks. Those who choose the phrase *one of the only,* for instance, may think they are conveying the same idea as that in *one of the few,* but they are merely contradicting themselves. Modifiers logically point to or emphasize the words nearest them. *My exact words* or *the very idea* or *that precise moment* could drop the emphasizing adjective and still make sense but might not serve the writer or speaker well.

Building a stronger vocabulary of adjectives and adverbs solves many wording problems. The user, however, needs an awareness not only of the meanings of modifiers but also of their associations. A dictionary gives a word's *denotation,* but its widespread implications are its *connotations.* The adjective *safe* has a denotative meaning of "secure, free from harm," but its connotations are among the most emotional of any word in the language, often producing images of happiness and home. Learning as much as possible about a word's connotative and denotative meanings will help determine the right modifier.

At the same time, be sure that phrases include all their needed modifiers. A television researcher for *Saturday Night Live* called with a frantic message. "We've checked all our dictionaries," she said, "and you are the last hope. We're planning a comedy sketch on superstitions, like not swimming for an hour after eating, so we tried looking up 'wives' tales.' Why can't we find an entry for that in the dictionary?" The answer, of course, was that the complete phrase was required; the term is "old wives' tales," and many dictionaries carry an entry under the term with its complete modifiers.

BARGAIN WITH JARGON

"I am not at liberty to say," a military leader says to sidestep a question. That well-worn naval phrase, *at liberty*, takes an extra word and several extra syllables to equal an easier word: *free*.

The trained ear can hear jarring jargon and replace it with simpler words. *Apparel* is a fashion term, almost always carrying a heavier weight than the simpler *clothes*. Similarly stuffy is the grammarian's *substantive*, easily replaced by the simpler *noun*.

Take time to find the easier word, even when more fanciful terms are available. At an East Coast amusement park with a Renaissance theme, the sign over one food stand showed regal names for the sandwiches. An unsuspecting patron tried to order according to the sign and asked for "a Henry IV burger" and "a Richard II platter." The waiter, not knowing his own company's jargon, stared back blankly, finally asking, "You want a what?"

Standard English provides the basic terms for communication. To that vocabulary, jargon or slang may be added in light measure. The speaker or writer must be sure, though, that the term being used will be clear in context; otherwise, an explanation must be offered as a bargain with jargon.

Legal language is particularly guilty of overexpressing the logical thought with its own brand of jargon, known as legalese. *Party of the first part* comes from contract law, and it is a verbal distancer. Those five words replace the party's name, which is frequently shorter than the phrase.

Remember that language changes; some slang words become Standard English, while others disappear. At this writing, the label of *brain surgeon* has given way to *rocket scientist* and may lead to *astrophysicist;* anybody unstable or unpredictable is no longer *a wild card* but instead *a loose cannon,* and a *bad attitude* is expressed as just an *attitude.* In current slang, *cool* is hot, *bad* is good, and *neat* is neither.

Abbreviations and foreign words can also be confusing, both in meaning and in pronunciation. With the proliferation of acronyms and abbreviations, the reader or listener is made to do too much of the work. Consider the many forms of "p.c." beyond *political correctness: postcard, personal computer, police chief, positively confusing.* Use an abbreviation only after the complete form has been given.

Foreign terms are no easier. The English noun *sale* is spelled the same as a French adjective that means "dirty," and the two versions of *sale* are pronounced differently. A century ago, Mark Twain commented on the dangers of trying to pronounce foreign words: "In Paris they just simply opened their eyes and stared when I spoke to them in French; I never did succeed in making those idiots understand their own language."

PLACE TERM LIMITS

Not only politicians should be concerned about the need for term limits. Every language user should be conscious of the length and built-in power of the words being chosen. "Short words are best," Winston Churchill said, "and the old words when short are best of all."

Writers and speakers alike should watch the length of words. Many people lose power in their language by reaching for the long word when a short one is better. A police officer, for example, wanted to describe the activity of a suspect before being arrested: "He was able to actualize himself up the tree but was not able to actualize himself down the tree." Replacing the four-syllable *actualize* with the one-syllable *climb* would lead to an instant increase in power. Longer is rarely if ever stronger, or English teachers would not deplore the use of *methodology* in place of *method* or *utilization* in place of *use*. The aim of keeping words short is to sound conversational, and conversation usually lags whenever listeners must contend with jarring uses of jargon.

Legalese has also helped stiffen the language. Business memos that once started with *regarding* or *about* now lead off with *pursuant to,* making the receiver (not the *recipient*) feel more like a litigant than a business contact. *Desirous* is another term that is longer, not stronger. The attorney who says, "My client *is desirous of testifying,*" lacks the power of conviction found in "My client *wants to testify.*"

Twain overcame the habit of extending words when he began to write for money. "An average English word is four letters and a half," he explained, adding, "I never write *metropolis* for seven cents, because I can get the same price for *city*. I never write *policeman,* because I can get the same money for *cop*."

Imagine being paid by the word, and the wastefulness of using longer words will fall away. Pressing the point, Twain concluded, "I never write *valetudinarian* at all, for not even hunger and wretchedness can humble me to the point where I will do a word like that for seven cents; I wouldn't do it for fifteen."

Many people lose power in their language by insisting on the long word when a short one will do. During the early nineteenth century, many American words, such as *confisticate* for *take* or *explaterate* for *explain*, added syllables and Latin endings to make words sound more scholarly. Today's communication needs the reverse process.

Knowing the audience helps. When lecturing to a group of scholars, a speaker may want to use the multisyllable words that introduced a recent article on literary scholarship: "Multiplicity, polysemy, plurivocality — those signs have become metonyms of late-twentieth-century postmodernity." Even in a lecture, however, long words tend to stifle rather than start the flow of language. To make language fit the occasion, word choice will still require educated guesswork — and a little common sense. "Scintillate, scintillate, minuscule asteroid" is not as powerful as "Twinkle, twinkle, little star."

Before choosing a modifier, make sure to consider the audience. A company published a brochure about the abilities of the *"in-house* facilities," provoking at least one writer to ask about the *"out-house* facilities." Always aim for a modifier that will elicit the right response; often the right modifier will be none at all: "facilities."

More often, though, modifiers lose the power to describe or to move because a longer word has displaced a stronger word. A survey of business leaders and professionals across the country yielded the following list of ten weak, underachieving adjectives. Watch for the weaker word, and consider the stronger alternative.

POWERING UP: MODIFIERS

"The committee has decided to take a proactive approach to the problem." (Clip *proactive* to the simpler *active.*)

"It is imperative that we act as quickly as possible to overcome the difficulty." (Rarely is *imperative* necessary; replace the first five words with *We must.*)

"An expeditious accounting may help avert future financial disaster." (Far faster than *expeditious* is *fast* or *quick.*)

"His version of the episode has proved to be fallacious." (A truer term for *fallacious* is *false* or *wrong*.)

"The length of time covered by the proposal was indeterminate." (Be clearer; use *vague* or *uncertain* in place of *indeterminate*.)

"The predominant characteristics should be noted and considered in future evaluations." (*Main* or *chief* expresses the same idea as *predominant*.)

"The Pentagon's equipment will be operational by the end of January." (*Ready* and *in use* are two ready replacements for *operational*.)

"A newer system will be introduced to replace the program that is dysfunctional." (The overworked *dysfunctional* may be fixed by using *broken* or *not working*.)

"No subsequent explanation has been offered for the incident." (*Later* is an acceptable replacement for *subsequent* if any adjective is even needed.)

"There has not been sufficient data for a decision to be reached." (Stow *sufficient*; *enough* is enough.)

5

INSPIRING WORDS

THE VERB IN ACTION

THE NEW YORK METS were not having a good day. Their first batter grounded out, according to the announcer, "and the second flew out to center field."

An amazed reader wrote to ask, "This can't be right, but can the past tense of *fly* ever be *flied?*" The answer depends on context. The past tense of *fly* is almost always *flew*, as in "The bird flew over the field." In baseball, though, *flied* is acceptable as the past tense of "to hit a fly ball." After a batter slugs the ball high over center field, never say that he *flew*, even if he plays for the Baltimore Orioles.

Verbs such as *fly* provide the vitality in sentences. Without verbs, no action takes place, and no explanations can be completed. The writer or speaker should always use verbs wisely and well, inspiring the audience to picture the words at play.

AIM FOR ACTION

Use active verbs whenever possible. *Go, work, reach, run* — every active verb pushes the meaning of the message along. Linking verbs are also necessary, as this sentence shows by using *are,* but nothing else moves words the way an active verb can.

Linking verbs, in comparison, contain no action or power beyond what *is* or *seems.* To say that *he is quick* is less forceful than to say that *he moves quickly,* and *she was the winner* always loses out to *she won.* Aim for action in the verb choice, and inspire the audience to envision the event being described or the explanation being offered.

Once that verb has been selected, however, other keys must be applied to make sure that it has the right form.

RECOGNIZE THE VERB'S VOICE

The television interviewer pushed his way into the house and apologized for interrupting the morning meal of his guests. "Why don't we set up breakfast in the kitchen," he said, "so your family is all ready to be eaten?" Unless cannibalism is the topic for the interview, the active infinitive *to eat* is more accurate here than the passive *to be eaten.*

In the active voice, the subject performs the action of the verb *(She earned a promotion).* The passive voice lacks that directness, pushing the object of the active voice *(promotion)* into the subject of the passive sentence; the passive verb phrase includes a form of *to be* and a past participle: *A promotion was earned by her.*

Which sentence performs better: "They called the police" or "The police were called by them"? Naturally, the first version sounds stronger and gets the point across faster. The second keeps the reader waiting for not only the action but also the ones performing the action. That sentence uses the passive voice, which turns the object of a strong sentence into the subject of a weak one.

Usually the writer or speaker should avoid the passive voice, for it often leads to vagueness or uncertainty. Passivity in *The contents were revealed* or *A decision was reached* removes the true subject from the action; it allows the speaker or writer to deny involvement or guilt, as in the State Department's use of *The judgment was delivered* or *Mistakes were made.* Equally weakened is any sentence using such distancing forms as "She found herself buying a new car" or "He was led to believe a lie," with verb phrases that shield their subjects from blame but also cut back on power.

LET HELPING VERBS HELP

Prefer a verb to a verb phrase. This generalization has its exceptions, but speakers and writers would do well to aim for a one-word verb to mark the action or condition they are describing. Each time a verb phrase is used, the power from a single-word verb is lost. The present tense *(I say)* carries more force than the present perfect *(I have said);* the simple *say* is also stronger than the forms of the present emphatic *(I do say)* and the present progressive *(I am saying).*

Helping verbs or auxiliaries shape or direct the action of the main verb. Try to stay out of the realm of mere possibility, though. A flight attendant announces, "Please check for any personal belongings you may have brought on board with you." Never mind what *you may have brought;* shorten it to *you brought.*

When using an auxiliary, watch out for its location in the sentence. Helping verbs do not help when they are placed incorrectly. Aim to be conversational in word placement, and avoid the stilted wording of *The decision finally was made.* The timely adverb would conversationally fall between the helping verb and the main part of the verb, as in *was finally made.*

The strength of helping verbs also requires the proper auxiliary. *Can* and *may* prove particularly troublesome to most word users, unaware or uncaring that *can* shows ability and *may* offers permission. A professor of business management writes to employees, "Your boss cannot ask you to do anything that is illegal." (A boss may not or should not but certainly *can* ask.) "You may have genius," commented Supreme Court Justice Oliver Wendell Holmes, adding, "The contrary is, of course, probable."

Too many auxiliaries can be more destructive than not enough. *That might would have been easier* should lose its *might* or *would* to express the idea more easily, and *This ought not should have happened* should also be rewritten. Fewer helping verbs will be more helpful.

CONTROL THE CONSISTENCY OF VERBS

For every verb chosen, consistency counts in tense, number, and mood.

A major problem with verbs is the consistency of tenses. Once a specific tense (past, present, future) has been chosen, the logical flow of the message requires the continued use of that tense, at least in the same paragraph. *He asked me a question and ignores the answer* creates a problem by mixing the past *(asked)* with the present *(ignores)*.

"Officials are optimistic that the government would approve the treaty soon" also shows tenses out of control. The present *are* and the near future implied by the adverb *soon* force the correct helping verb after *government* to be the future *will*, not the past or conditional *would*. A similar error occurs in "I didn't know what the word *meant*." Unless the meaning has changed, the correct wording is "what the word *means*," because it still holds true.

Even with consistent tenses, the right form of the verb is still necessary. Describing a case of mistaken identity, a television reporter said, "Maybe she mistaked her for someone else." The proper past tense is *mistook; mistaked* is a mistake. Regional or substandard verbs should be kept to a minimum. Questioned about property lost in a fire, a college student tells a judge, "Most were things I'd boughten myself"; the stunned judge replies, "You tell me you're going to college, and you use *boughten?*"

Also dangerous is the consistency of number (singular or plural) when verbs are introduced. With two or more subjects provided, the proper verb must be plural: "The House and the Senate are voting." Reversing the syntax makes no difference. "There *has* to be safeguards," says a banker, who should number his verbs more carefully: "There have to be safeguards." The ability to separate singular from plural will mark the speaker as somebody who handles words properly.

Moods also mark power language. English has only three moods for its verbs, each with its own strengths and weaknesses. Most of the time, a writer or speaker uses the indicative mood, stating something as a fact or expressing an idea in a straightforward sentence combining subject and verb.

Even more forceful is the imperative mood, used to give a command or make a suggestion. This mood assumes that the subject is already known. "Take a hike," an upset cab driver shouts at a poor tipper; the subject *(you)* does not need to be expressed.

Probably the least forceful mood is the subjunctive, which is disappearing from the language and trips up most of its would-be users. This mood, reserved for wishes and statements that are contrary to fact, now shows up mainly in set expressions. *Be that as it may* and *if I were you* (not *if I was you,* because it is contrary to fact) exemplify this mood in modern wording, but the subjunctive is frequently misused and must be carefully handled.

Long verbs are not necessarily strong verbs. The poet Oliver Wendell Holmes, Sr., father of the Supreme Court justice, pointed this out in a lecture about medical words more than a century ago. "I would never use a long word where a short one would answer the purpose," he said. "I know there are professors in this country who *ligate* arteries. Other surgeons only *tie* them, and it stops the bleeding just as well."

Watch how three sets of verbs grow in power as they shrink in syllables:

initiate — introduce — begin — start

accentuate — emphasize — highlight — stress

communicate — dialogue — discuss — talk

Extending other verbs by adding the suffix *-ize* also creates unnecessarily long words; writers and speakers should minimize the *-ize.*

Among the most useful active verbs is *say* (never to be confused with *go*). This simple verb carries its own weight and needs no embellishing to enlarge its meaning. Ponderous adverbs add little to its force; *he says inquisitively* or *she says energetically* should be used sparingly. Even worse is the overload of verbs designed to replace *say* with such extended forms as *interject* and *indicate.* Keep to the simple *say* — enough said.

The sentences below contain verbs likely to detract from the power of a message. After each example is the suggestion of one or more synonyms that can strengthen the intended meaning. Simplicity and action combine in many of these inspiring verbs.

POWERING UP: VERBS

"The lessons are designed to orientate the newcomers to procedure and practices." (The shorter *prepare* or the even shorter *orient* is a better choice than *orientate.*)

"A candidate's campaign literature insists, 'We must prioritize our objectives and stick to our convictions.'" (*Rate* or *rank* is preferable to *prioritize.*)

"The customers chose to purchase the more expensive furniture." (Sell short on the longer *purchase,* and instead buy into *buy.*)

"Whatever events transpire in the meantime, the company will be fiscally prepared." (Both *happen* and *occur* are shorter, and neither carries the stuffiness of *transpire.*)

"The Treasury idea would make the trustee securitize the debt." (Be secure with the simpler verb *secure.*)

"Smaller committees will be formed to implement the suggestions of the board." (Try implementing the easier *carry out* or even *act on* instead of *implement.*)

"Group leaders will be expected to elucidate the details of the plan." (To make words more lucid, drop *elucidate* in favor of *explain* or *tell.*)

"Prospective employees would benefit from the chance to network with managers of similar companies." (The overused *network* should be condensed to *meet* or at least *make contact.*)

"Without an opportunity to interface with other consumers, the users of this product will be unable to evaluate its quality." (Usually *interface* means nothing more than *talk,* sometimes *exchange views.*)

"The early communications have allowed us to facilitate an early resolution to the strike." (Easier words for *facilitate* include *ease* or *help.*)

"The members of the board have felt pressurized by the demands of the stockholders." (The British verb *pressurize* is longer than the American *pressure* and should be clipped.)

"Our intention is to service the customer as quickly as possible." (Speed up even more by shortening the double-edged *service* to the single-syllable *serve.*)

"She intended to instigate a thorough examination of the review process." (Start replacing *instigate* with *begin* or *start.*)

"His pointed comments merely served to exacerbate the friction in the office." (Get to the point faster than *exacerbate* does; use *make worse* or *intensify.*)

"The rebate offer will expire the last day of December." (End the stuffiness of *expire* with *end* or even *die.*)

6

STRONG WORDS

EMPOWERING NOUNS

IN THE 1950 film *Sunset Boulevard,* Gloria Swanson plays the reclusive Norma Desmond, a star of silent films trying to renew her career in the age of talkies. Norma knows what she likes. When the word *comeback* is mentioned to her, she bristles: "I hate that word. It's *return* — a return to the millions of people who've never forgiven me for deserting the screen."

Some words are stronger than others. The connotations of nouns can make all the difference, and to Norma the negative *comeback* fell far short of the uplifting *return. Comeback* suggested a decline, followed by starting over; *return* suggested a voluntary departure, with no hint of failure. Other nouns are similarly controlled by connotation.

Home, for example, carries a weight and resonance that *residence* and *domicile* will never house, just as *altercation* lacks the punch of *fight.* Many powerful words are nouns, but that power must be released through careful use to capture the word's connotations, not always found in a dictionary. Fans of jazz will agree with Louis Armstrong's assessment: "If you have to ask what jazz is, you'll never know." Another popular term is *vacation,* and any vacation that does not allow the mind and body to vacate, in the original sense of the word, weakens the identity of the noun.

As identifiers of people, places, and things, nouns mark the subject and object of any action. The ability to use these words well will separate the forceful phrasers from the weak. Exercising the right noun, though, presents several obstacles, each of which must be overcome in the quest for power language. Choosing the wrong noun, or using the right noun weakly, can harm an argument and eliminate its effectiveness. Aiming for the strongest noun possible will improve the argument and force the words around that noun to work equally hard.

NAME NAMES

In an age of product identity and designer labels, specific names hold power. The ability to catch the audience's attention with the proper name is an asset not to be ignored. That asset, however, should not be exploited, at least not to the point of saturation.

Identifying a specific house as the White House or as Elvis Presley's Graceland will trigger images in a listener's mind that the plain *house* lacks. Similarly, a person's name is almost always more effective than an unlabeled description; the name provides a handle for the audience to hold and recall throughout a story or discussion. Not having that name can cause the listener to wonder whether the story is fictitious or even whether the speaker or writer is the unnamed subject.

Whenever a generic noun is being used, more power may be added to the term by using the definite article *the.* Film titles, from *The Terminator* to *The Fugitive,* use *the* to point to a specific character. Demonstrative words such as *this* and *that* can also be powerful indicators, more forceful than the use of the indefinite articles, *a* or *an.* In the nineteenth century,

Charles Dickens could get away with the general or indefinite article in such titles as *A Tale of Two Cities* or *A Christmas Carol.* Nowadays, though, the specified example almost always overpowers the generic.

CLEAN UP NOUN CLUTTER

More power pulsates from a single noun than from a noun cluster. The practice of pushing nouns together, forming long strings of substantives, leads from noun cluster to noun clutter. Referring to a city by placing its name before *area* is a clear case of noun clutter; nothing happens in the Washington area unless it happens in Washington. In the same way, not every problem should be labeled a specific *syndrome* (football's "postconcussion syndrome") or *thing* (George Bush's "vision thing").

The problem becomes far more serious when three or more nouns are piled together to express an idea. Scientists and politicians are notorious for these word clusters that are too often demeaning to meaning. "Health care" uses *health* as an attributive noun to describe *care;* the longer "health care reform" pushes the limit of noun clutter, and "health care reform proposals" goes over the edge, along with "health care service products." Dodge promotes its "available integrated child safety seats," and a church group announces "the Washington West District United Methodist Men's Prayer Breakfast." An advertisement in the entertainment newspaper *Variety* is headlined "The World's Single Largest Contemporary Chinese Language Film Library."

Sometimes the clutter is indecipherable. Consider the phrase "Joint Protection Principles." Does it come from an arthritis pamphlet or a defense manual? Only the word user knows for certain unless the context (such as a military guide) makes the meaning clear.

PREFER THE NORMAL TO THE FORMAL

Even Winnie the Pooh suffered from this syndrome. When the owl talks to him of "customary procedure" in A. A. Milne's story, it is more than Winnie can bear. "'What does Crustimoney Proseedcake mean?' said Pooh. 'For I am a Bear of Very Little Brain, and long words Bother me.'"

Among the shortest and most powerful words are pronouns. Look to *it* to avoid repetition of the same noun or elegant variation (silver as "the precious metal"). Those who introduce speakers should be especially aware of the power in pronouns. If the speaker's name will cause applause, the introducer may want to withhold it until the end of the introduction. It is possible to substitute *he* or *she* throughout the introduction, building to the name of the speaker at the end of the remarks.

When a pronoun will not do, use a noun that everybody will understand. Word watchers have long been impressed by the capacity of English to contain an exact word for almost everything, from fear of talking (laliophobia) to fear of the color red (erythrophobia). Using those long words, however, stifles the message unless they are clearly explained in the context. A big vocabulary may impress, but it may not express. (The exception would be a scholarly audience that understands — and expects — erudite discourse.)

Also, watch out for suffix suffocation. Wordwise, the poorest of all suffix forms is *-wise.* A charity worker says, "We gave back volunteer-wise." A singles group worries about the future "relationship-wise," while a politician tries to rebuild "staff-wise." Rarely does a noun benefit from this addition, used wisely by Benjamin Franklin two centuries ago. "Some are weatherwise," he wrote; "some are otherwise." In fact, almost any suffix helps suffocate the noun it appends; this tendency to let the ends of words grow in length draws strength away from their message.

Advertisers have found the opposite to be true with a prefix, where "the bigger, the better" is the order. Starting words off with *super-* and *mega-* and *ultra-* lends importance to otherwise plain products; packagers know the value of size, with some movie popcorn sold in boxes marked *large* for the smallest available. Just as action counts for verbs, implying size makes nouns more powerful.

The wrong prefix or suffix, however, can cause extensive weakening of the message. An Amtrak announcer on a slow train kept apologizing for the *unconvenience,* using a choice of prefix that was "infortunate." Make sure to select the right affix for the intended word, but first consider whether one is needed: *Pre-* adds nothing to *prearrange or prepaid.*

Will prefixes be downsized and suffix suffocation be stopped? The best answer comes from Sam Goldwyn, the movie mogul. "In two words," Goldwyn is reputed to have said, "im possible."

Studying the way people talk when they are not self-conscious about their words may be the easiest way to discover strong nouns and inspiring verbs. Some words show force all by themselves; when a fierce protest was first called a *firestorm* or a verbal attack was referred to as a *bashing,* these words offered powerful images that could be seen and understood. Helping the reader or listener with visual words is a major goal of power language.

Always exercise strong nouns and vital verbs. Such verbs as *twist* and *ignite* add action or provide excitement. Similarly, strong nouns name specific things that can be visualized or trigger emotional reactions; *car* is better than the general *vehicle* (though not so rich as *Jaguar* or *Corvette*), and *occupation* is never so strong as *work.* Flex a muscular vocabulary, emphasizing strong words that capture the interest and imagination of the audience.

The sentences that follow include nouns in need of empowering. Keep in mind, though, that words do change their meanings over time. *Cattle,* for instance, began as a general term in Middle English for "movable property"; over the centuries, the term was restricted to livestock, and for today's English speakers any sense but "cows" makes no sense.

POWERING UP: NOUNS

"The concert has been moved to a smaller venue because of slow ticket sales." (Replace the formal *venue* with the common word *place* or *site*.)

"Four of the prisoners have been granted a special schedule of visitation privileges." (The shorter *visiting* is enough in place of *visitation*.)

"Without a proper closure, the story seems unsatisfying and perhaps structurally weak." (The psychology cliché of *closure*, which moved into literary criticism and then the general language, offers little that *close* or *ending* lacks.)

"The modality of the operations never seems to be simplified for the users." (Simplify *modality* to *mode* or at least *method*.)

"Government supervisors have tried to limit the expenditure under the current budget." (Try also to limit *expenditure* to the simpler *spending*.)

"Several characters are drawn into the jealousness of the title character for her rival." (Watch the unnecessary use of -ness, especially with the common *jealousy* already available for *jealousness*.)

"Youngness appeared clearly in the policeman's face." (Here -ness adds an unnecessary syllable, and *youngness* should be dropped for *youth*.)

"The program was praised for its presentation and comprehensiveness." (The same range of meaning in *comprehensiveness* may be found in *range* or *scope*.)

"Participants tried to maintain the same objective during the process." (Aim to replace *objective* with the simpler *aim* or *goal*.)

"At least one subordinate was called back into the office to help with the revisions." (Only *aide* or *helper* is needed, not *subordinate.*)

"The new product was considered for any other possible utilization." (Possible replacements for *utilization* include *use* and *purpose.*)

"Without the supportiveness of colleagues, he knew the work would not have been completed by the deadline." (*Help* or *aid* may be enough to replace *supportiveness,* and certainly no more than *support* is needed.)

"The company considered his proclivity toward recklessness before he was hired." (Either *tendency* or *leaning* would be a better choice than *proclivity.*)

"Try this new baby formulation." (This advertisement for a baby formula would do better with the simpler *formula.*)

"There was too much of a discrepancy there for the competition to overcome." (Differ from users of *discrepancy* by trying *difference* or *contrast.*)

"Factory workers were warned about the possibilities of injuriation during the difficult activity." (No injury is done by shortening *injuriation* to the proper *injury.*)

"Management questioned the functionality of the equipment when it was introduced." (Here the long noun *functionality* means nothing more than *usefulness* or even *use.*)

"He was described as a paradigm for other workers in the company." (If *ideal* or *model* is meant, either is stronger than the overworked *paradigm.*)

"The Department of Health issued a notice of violation regarding limit exceedances." (*Exceedances* exceeds the limit; change it to the simpler *excesses.*)

"Implementation of the new machinery is expected to ease the workload of most employees." (Use the simpler *use* in place of *implementation.*)

7

HONEST WORDS

LOW-IMPACT LANGUAGE

E UPHEMISM, the ultimate form of meekspeak, once had an important function. When a writer or speaker wished to avoid offending or insulting, a euphemistic term would be substituted. Today, though, euphemism is everywhere, bloating the language with dishonest words.

"His response has a credibility gap" avoids *lie,* and "Catch a classic episode of the television series tonight" avoids *rerun.* Similarly, *Department of Kinetic Wellness* is what a high school in Wisconsin calls its physical education program, and a trailer park is now glorified as a *mobile home resort.* The subject of English in many schools is no longer *English;* instead, it has become *language arts.* Even the simple *library* has been stretched, becoming a *media resource center.*

The use of inflated language is not the honest mistake of choosing the wrong word. When a guest on a radio talk show spoke of his youth and a lasting "childish dream of visiting Australia," he misspoke, substituting *childish* ("foolish") for *childhood* (a word that points back to the user's younger days). Euphemism, however, is deliberate and often dishonest.

This generation may be witnessing the passing away of honest language. In a crowded grocery store, a perplexed customer stops the manager next to the fruits and vegetables. "What's the difference," the customer asks, "between a yam and a sweet potato?" The manager pauses to think and finally answers, "Eight cents a pound."

Truth lurks in that old joke about the difference in naming, and that truth is based on the power of euphemism. Nothing is sold *used* anymore; even old wrecks of cars have taken the high road to being labeled *preowned.* If the new name suggests a higher quality, all the better, says the seller. Even *honest* implies something less than honest; restaurants now offer "soup made fresh from honest ingredients."

This Humpty Dumpty approach to language — a word means just what the user chooses — also requires a gullible audience, willing to accept whatever meaning the speaker or writer assigns to a word. (The same audience has probably been fooled by the comment "The word *gullible* isn't in the dictionary.") Without that implicit acceptance of a twisted meaning, the new term remains meaningless. Compared with words used for their true meanings, euphemism always forfeits its power.

EXPRESS TERMS HONESTLY

The twentieth century has been an age of euphemism. In 1929, the writer Paul Richard commented, "The vagabond, when rich, is called a tourist." Soon the floodgate opened.

When Dwight Eisenhower gave his State of the Union Address in 1960, he questioned the new way of words: "We live ... in a sea of semantic disorder in which old labels no longer faithfully describe," the president said. "Police states are called 'people's democracies.' Armed conquest of free people is called 'liberation.'"

Politicians no longer want to raise taxes; instead, health care is to be paid for by *premiums.* Even the taxpayer is no longer so called. Check the fine print in the bulletins of the Internal Revenue Service, in which taxpayers are now referred to as "valued customers." That term implies voluntary business, but trying not to do business with the IRS is a crime.

Historically, some euphemisms have proved more useful than others. The delicacy of discussing death has given way to *passed away* or even the confusing *gone*. Less helpful was the Victorian era's use of *piano limbs* to avoid mentioning *legs*, just as *cashmere perspirer* is no improvement on the actual *sweater*. No other euphemism, however, can touch the mistaken impression created by *buy the farm*; that euphemism for *die*, as in "He just bought the farm," can be misunderstood, suggesting the recently deceased is still alive and dealing in real estate.

STRENGTHEN WEAK TERMS

Lucille Ball knew the humor in avoiding certain words. In an episode of *I Love Lucy*, she banters with her husband about using coercion to get her own way; he calls it blackmail. "Oh, let's not call it that," she responds. He repeats that it is still blackmail. "I know," Lucy agrees, "but let's not *call* it that."

Hiding behind euphemism is a sure way to make readers and listeners upset with the word user. Dishonest language appears so frequently that candid words become refreshing. Two years ago, the media celebrated a Virginia judge who reversed an earlier decision, adding the straightforward statement "I was *wrong*." That adjective carried more blunt force than *incorrect* or *mistaken*, strengthened by its shortness.

Many weak euphemisms have shorter, stronger counterparts. *Layoffs* or cutting the work force should not be hidden as *downsizing* or *rightsizing*, and shrinking the number of workers is definitely not *miniaturizing*. Losing a job is not pleasant, no matter the name given to the process, and such weakness in word usage may lead the audience to wonder what else in the message is meant to remain hidden or unclear.

Sometimes writers and speakers twist the message on purpose. The use of hyperbole — deliberate overstatement — is found in any scheme labeled "Get rich quick!" Writers choose hyperbole for comic effect; when Shirley Jackson wrote of the humor in rearing four children, she used inflated terms to call those misadventures *Life Among the Savages* and *Raising Demons.*

Advertisers are especially adept at putting the hype into hyperbole. Overstatement can leave an audience skeptical, however, when every product is *new and improved* and *recommended most.* Similarly, the language is inflated when each passing rain shower is labeled "one of the worst storms in years"; even if the storm is severe, "a severe storm" does not need to be stretched into hyperbole — unless, of course, there are facts to back up the stronger statement.

The reverse of hyperbole is meiosis, also known as understatement. When the British first referred to the Atlantic Ocean as "the Pond," there was force in understating. Now, though, meiosis leans toward the dishonest ("Some assembly required") if not the outright lie ("The check is in the mail"). Be vigilant in finding terms that do not mislead.

FLATTEN INFLATED TERMS

Inflation seems to have taken over the language. Not every success is a *monster.* Not every performer is a *superstar,* nor every model a *supermodel.* Even the *information superhighway* has an inflated name. Advertisers give *an incredible discount* or try to lure customers with *a fabulous offer,* asking consumers to believe a discount that is not believable or accept an offer that should appear only in fables.

The simple *diet* has been unnecessarily stretched to *food program* and recently widened to *personal weight management.* A crime once known as a *felony* tries to masquerade today as a *felonious criminal incident.* In sheer force, a single word almost always outweighs a euphemistic phrase, but not when the word is inflated: Burger King has raised the person who takes the order and makes change from a *cashier* to an *expeditor.*

One sure way to flatten inflated terms is to remember the roots of words, the basis for their current meanings. *Astonishing* has become the usual synonym for *surprising;* the adjective *astonishing* comes from the Latin *tonere,* meaning "to thunder," and the accurate user of *astonishing* should feel the effect of being "thunderstruck."

Not every offer is *once in a lifetime,* nor every discount *out of this world.* Putting too much weight into modifiers for every-day words may inflate the meaning to the bursting point. Try instead to find exact nouns and verbs that require few modifiers to clarify the meaning.

In 1994, the federal government finally dropped its poorest designation of workers: *essential employees.* During winter storms in past years, Washington shut down except for the defense and safety workers who were considered crucial to the city's maintenance. Each winter the call went out for *essential employees,* an inflated term with the insulting implication that the majority of government workers are not essential. A better term was needed, and the government's choice was finally apt: *emergency workers.*

Inflate the values of words, and risk miscommunicating the message. *Euphemism* comes from the Greek roots for "good speaking," but the best speaking makes the message clear and honest. Insist on true meaning as much as possible, and audiences will come to trust the message as well as the messenger.

The ultimate word on euphemisms should be that the normal word almost always outpowers the formal word. Take *ultimate,* which may be replaced by *final,* which may be replaced by *last.* Knowing when to be formal and when to be forceful can help any writer or speaker overcome the urge to blur or inflate.

Watch the wording in the following sentences. Each example

of euphemism may lead to humor or at least obscured language. Being specific is the surest way to eliminate (or *end*) the use of euphemism.

DEFLATING LANGUAGE

"The gentleman robbing the bank escaped the police." (Ignore the urge to elevate every man to *gentleman* or every woman to *lady*; often, as in this case, the result sounds ridiculous.)

"The field is not to be populated." (Computer users and form writers have come to expect this wordy version of "Leave the space blank.")

"Throughout the guitar concert, chords were digitally operated." (The review means to say "chords were *fingered.*")

"I'm an insect psychologist, a holistic pest-control technician." (This exterminator was having fun with the term *exterminator*, just as housewives have become *domestic engineers* and janitors are *sanitation engineers*.)

"We refer to those second showings as *encore performances.*" (A *rerun* by any other name, including *classic episode*, still looks the same.)

"The government is planning to introduce a new revenue enhancement." (This announcement normally follows a political promise of "no new taxes.")

"Incidental casualties have not yet been assessed." (Behind this military jargon is the reality of *innocent victims.*)

"During his career as a criminal, he burglarized hundreds of houses." (Burglary does not qualify as a *career*; try *years* or *time.*)

"We will be softening our prices 25 percent." (*Softening* is *lowering*; when prices go back up, will they be *hardening*?)

"His entrepreneurial endeavor will come to fruition in the next month or so." (A *new business* will soon be opening.)

"The medical booklet suggests that you consult your provider of care if you have questions." (This medical authority used to be called a *doctor.*)

"Next month we expect to be rightsizing our work force." (Employees should be prepared for the company's *downsizing,* another euphemism for *layoffs.*)

"The music store offers the assistance of customer sales counselors." (A *clerk* will try to help.)

"Headquarters are expected to be fully operational next month." (This inflation means *ready* or *working.*)

"For further recipes, please consult with our food service specialist." (Consider this phrase a meekspeak version of *cook.*)

II

POWER LINES

HOW TO USE WORDS

8

WORDING

FIT PHRASING

IN 1776, the signers of the Declaration of Independence knew that their dangerous words could prove fatal. At that momentous juncture in the American Revolution, Ben Franklin turned to encourage his fellow conspirators. "We must all hang together," he reminded them, "or assuredly we shall all hang separately."

Words, like conspirators, must "hang together." Gathered into strong phrases, the right words can make the meaning clear and communicate the idea efficiently. Made to work separately or without the force of proper phrasing, the same words may harm the message.

A phrase is any group of words that has no verb or fails to offer a complete idea. Phrases take various forms, from prepositional phrases *(over the river and through the woods)* to infinitive phrases *(to be or not to be)*. Finding the best ways to join single words into memorable phrases will set apart the communications by any writer or speaker.

SHORTEN LONG PHRASES

Among the fastest keys to power language is the expression once used by the British poet Robert Browning: "Less is more." Remember that advice. The more words used to communicate an idea, the more chances to lose the attention of the audience. Look at that concluding phrase, *the attention of the audience,* and see how much more direct it is in a shorter form: *the audience's attention.* Phrases that start with *of* are known as periphrastic — that is, they take a roundabout way to express a short idea. "The films of Steven Spielberg" is almost always less effective than "Steven Spielberg's films," especially when *films* should be emphasized. The roundabout, or periphrastic, form works better to emphasize the object of the preposition, in this case Steven Spielberg. Make sure that the long phrase works in favor of the meaning, that it does not just increase the length of the sentence.

One of the wordy phrases for lengthening the language is *one of the.* Watch how changing that phrase to the simple article *a* saves time and energy. A wordy phrase should be compressed whenever possible; the shorter form will pass along the message sooner.

Shortened phrases must still convey the same idea, though. To compress "the time of my life" into "my lifetime" does justice to neither phrase. "My lifetime" covers a time period, while "the time of my life" suggests a highlight of that period.

Also, do not choose a single word over a phrase if the meaning will vary. "He mails only four letters a day" does not mean the same thing as "He mails as few as four letters a day"; with *only,* four letters are sent each day, but *as few as* offers the possibility of more than four. The search for stronger wording should never change the meaning. An introduction to *Omni Gazetteer* reports a headline about the marriage of a groom from Peculiar, Missouri, and a bride from Oblong, Illinois. Compressed too much, the headline announced PECULIAR MAN MARRIES OBLONG GIRL. A similar error beset a Maryland power company, which designated one of its executives the "vice president for gas."

Often a series of short phrases may be combined if not removed. "In the middle of the air" sounds stilted and forced in place of "in midair." That shorter, more precise wording saves the reader or listener from four unnecessary words and hastens the message.

Forceful phrasing takes practice, particularly in linking words that will have the maximum impact with minimum effort. Far too often, the phrases chosen add little or no information to the message being expressed. Wordiness depletes power.

FINISH PARTIAL PHRASES

The headline stood out: PIZZA FORGER FACES CHARGE. Was somebody forging pizzas? No, the article explained, the forger was passing bad checks at pizza parlors. The partial phrase only confused the reader.

A cookbook that offers "recipes sure to please the biggest appetites and everything in between" also lacks a completed idea. The phrase "everything in between" implies that more than one point has been considered. In this case, however, "the smallest appetites" has not been included to allow a space for the "in between." Be sure that every idea is explained enough to make the phrases comprehensible.

Worse are the word pictures in obvious need of completion. A safety warning about underground parking garages points out, "Someone can easily hide in between a car." Either another car or a wall or something is needed to complete that picture of hiding; remember that the root of *between* is *two*, and two objects are always needed.

Other and *else* are crucial words for completing phrases of comparison. The phrase that refers to the new car that goes faster "than any car" contradicts itself by suggesting the new car is not a car; try "than any other car." Any advertisement that states "Nothing works better" would better serve its product with "Nothing else works better."

Another error is the shorthand form of *as far as*. A chef announces, "As far as dinner, there will be a choice of main courses." The phrase starting that sentence should be a full clause: "As far as dinner is concerned." Anything less is incomplete.

"I am not unhappy," says a character in a play. The audience is left to wonder whether that means the character is happy. Wordiness is not power, and the widespread introduction of *not un-* depletes strength.

The Greeks had a word for this extensive use of the double negative: litotes (*lite*-uh-teez). A person who seems vaguely familiar may be described as "not unfamiliar," just as a possible action is considered "not impossible." A New Jersey government document makes the comment that "A finding of *not inconsistent* is the same as a finding of *consistent*." These gentler ways of expressing a positive through two negatives have the effect of producing understatement or allowing something that may be unpopular or unkind to be expressed in a circular form.

Roundabout wording is not powerful. Listen to the comment of a marine interviewed on *60 Minutes* about sexism in the service: "I'd be a liar if I said there wasn't." Sometimes, of course, that type of expression may be useful, especially in expressing ideas that will hurt, but power language should usually forgo circularity in favor of bluntness. Expressing the idea directly allows the speaker or writer to be not misunderstood.

More often, a double negative is seen as a simple error, trying to emphasize the negativity through the sheer force of negative words. That negative sense sometimes connects opposing words, creating an oxymoron, frequently equated with a contradiction in terms.

A fine line exists, though, between *oxymoron* and *contradiction in terms*. The longer expression is more encompassing, suggesting that two or more opposing terms are used together, with or without meaning. When a television character explains, "The reason for this meeting is mutual self-interest," the meaning is lost between *mutual* (which means "reciprocal") and *self-interest* (which cannot be reciprocated by another person). Similarly, the preacher who asks the pianist to "play silently" during a baptismal ceremony is asking the impossible. An *oxymoron*, however, joins two opposing terms into something understandable, no matter how contradictory the notion may seem at first. When Romeo leaves Juliet in Shakespeare's play, she sighs, "Parting is such sweet sorrow." The sadness of *sorrow* yoked to the adjective *sweet* depicts the mingled emotion of parting in an oxymoron.

The modern oxymoron is used on occasion to form humor aimed at a specific group. Comedians point to the oxymoron in "postal service" or "military intelligence." Below are kinder examples of this technique, pushing together two or more unlikely word partners.

THE OXYMORON

"The track will be offering even odds on the favored horse this weekend" pairs *even* and *odds.*

"Designers of the new entertainment complex hope to provide serious fun for future generations" combines *serious* and *fun.*

"The price for jumbo shrimp has steadily increased in recent years" links *jumbo* and *shrimp.*

"Her performance is the only blessing in an otherwise memorably forgettable film" adds *memorably* to *forgettable.*

"Please provide the office with the original as well as an original duplicate of the document" mixes *original* and *duplicate.*

"Partygoers seemed stunned into thunderous silence at the entrance of the unexpected couple" describes *silence* as *thunderous.*

"They may not have paid for the work, but they offered free transportation and food — same difference" adds *same* to *difference.*

"More adult children are finding themselves caregivers for their aging parents" links *adult* and *children.*

"The newspaper office has no explanation for the copies that have shown up missing after the morning delivery" mixes *shown up* and *missing.*

"Dancers who have complained about the constriction of movement have been offered loose tights" combines *loose* and *tights.*

"The leaders of Parliament may expect the loyal opposition to have the same dubious reaction" adds *loyal* to *opposition.*

"SENATE RETREATS AHEAD was spotted as a recent headline in the publication" yokes *retreats* and *ahead.*

"All participants should be warned that cancellation of the event is a firm possibility" joins *firm* and *possibility.*

9

REWORDING

SLOW WORDS AT WORK

"RUSH HOUR" NEVER seems to live up to its name. The traffic in front begins to thicken and slow down, finally crawling to a stop. Eventually, bumper to bumper, the cars inch past a construction area where everybody seems to be on a break, and the flashing lights illuminate the only sign: SLOW MEN AT WORK.

The double meaning of that message may draw a smile or a groan, depending on the mood of the driver. Words often have that two-sided effect, when the term can be read in more than a single way. Another traffic sign promises a rare sight: CHILDREN CROSSING 30 MILES PER HOUR. Twice the meaning, however, can mean half the sense, and power is lost whenever the audience must stop to consider both the intended meaning and an unintentional possibility for the same phrase.

Questions about clarity slow down the communication, blocking the passage of meaning and leading to massive message mix-ups.

SPEED UP SLOW WORDS

Sometimes a single word or the lack of a punctuation mark can delay communication. In the traffic sign, a dash or colon after *slow* or *crossing* would prevent misreading.

Other times, however, the choice of a word may cause the meaning to be harmed. Long and unfamiliar words are especially culpable; the audience unfamiliar with *culpable* may deduce the meaning from its context, but speakers or writers who use unfamiliar words should be prepared to offer as much help as necessary for understanding. Defining the word in the midst of using it is one possibility; another is to clarify the surrounding message so that no misunderstanding may occur.

A contestant on a game show was offered a prize for using *hypothesis* in a sentence. Her attempt — "He became famous for his hypothesis" — was accepted, even though it lacked any sense of the word's meaning. Try alternative terms, from *hypodermia* to *hippopotamus*, in the same sentence, and the meaning is no clearer.

Omitting a word such as *that* is often a power move, but that word is not always dispensable. Take the sentence that begins a science fiction film: "Many Americans believed visitors from outer space had actually landed." Without *that*, it is possible to misread it momentarily as "Many Americans believed visitors from outer space"; with *that*, there can be no misreading: "Many Americans believed that visitors from outer space had actually landed."

STRAIGHTEN OUT MIXED MESSAGES

- The front door of a major news bureau has a sign with this greeting: "Welcome to the bureau. The door is locked."
- A brand of security doors marked "This door is alarmed" may alarm its readers.

- A Washington politician comments, "Every single person is concerned about taxes," and is immediately asked how married people will respond.

Occasionally a word or phrase may send out conflicting meanings that need to be unscrambled for the message to be clear. A newspaper headline states RUNAWAY HOME, but the reader must check the article to learn whether it covers a house for runaways or the return of a single runaway. Allowing the double meaning to stand will cause problems not only for the word user but also for the audience. Deciding on the proper meaning and choosing words that clarify the sense will do much to make language more powerful.

A mail-order firm advertises, "Write to us if you need movie soundtracks. Good luck!" That parting phrase, trying to wish the customer well, suggests the second sense of "don't waste your time." A line of dialogue in a detective novel is equally vague: "You can't know too much about the men you're working for these days." Be careful that the chosen words offer only one meaning and say what is meant.

The possibility of misreading can lead to strange or humorous wording. David Letterman probably welcomed the double reading of his "stupid pet tricks," but some animal lovers have objected. A newspaper article on a Russian count speculates, "He might have married Grace Kelly instead of Prince Rainier of Monaco." It took a moment for readers to take in that gossip; turn that mixed message around to make it clear that "Grace Kelly might have married him instead of Prince Rainier."

SINGLE OUT DOUBLE MEANINGS

Occasionally, though, a double meaning is useful. The owner of a construction firm was dumbfounded when his neighbors decided to build a new house overshadowing his property. Asked by the neighbors for his opinion of their new home, he wanted to express his dismay without directly offending them. Finally, the right word came to him: *Imposing,* he said, using both its senses of "impressive" and "intrusive." Whenever a double meaning is possible, set apart the word or phrase as much as possible to allow its force to be felt.

Unlike the construction executive, who needed a word with two senses, most speakers and writers do well to aim for one specific sense in a word. Multiple meanings, useful in some contexts, may confuse or distort the message in others. The sign PROFESSIONALLY DRIVEN on the side of a truck may describe either the careful vehicle or its ambitious driver. Similarly, a Janus word such as *oversight* can suggest either the positive "overseeing" or the negative "overlooking"; the White House must be tired of jokes about its Intelligence Oversight Board.

English is filled with easily mistaken expressions, from "gross earnings" to "dressing a chicken." With two meanings for many terms, the language may seem impossible to interpret literally; the court system tries to do it, but problems occur. After a verdict was handed in, the judge turned to the jury and inquired, "So say you one, so say you all?" More than one jury member replied, "You all."

A character on a television drama tells a doctor, "I have a few questions I'd like to ask myself." In the unlikely event that she wants to ask herself questions, she need not bother the doctor; the reflexive pronoun *myself* should either be dropped or moved closer to the *I* it emphasizes: "I myself have a few questions." On the same show, another character says, "I'm not the one doing the hurting around here." Whether she was talking about hurting herself or hurting others was not made clear.

Double entendre does have its deliberate uses. Advertising copywriters, for example, know how to make double meanings work to advantage. The home appliances by Whirlpool are deftly advertised: "How to make a home run."

Cutting down on double talk, though, takes practice. A mother and her young son were arguing about his visit to the dentist the next day. Tired of his complaining, the mother thought she would settle the matter by exclaiming, "You're going to the dentist tomorrow, and don't you open your mouth!" Her son, of course, agreed.

Straighten out mixed messages by making sure that what is said cannot be misunderstood. A newspaper feature says of its subject, "She had an awful lunch yesterday," without explaining whether the lunch was bad or simply too large. The passages below contain words that are slow, some downright lethargic, in expressing the intended meaning. Each example is followed by at least one way to reword it for more power.

Remember that double plays on words and names may lend power to prose, if the reference is clear. Comics have long used "Walk this way" to introduce a Jerry Lewis stride, while "Call me a taxi" asks for assistance, not name calling. Humorists hone their power by waiting for the appropriate moment to spring their traps. The more unexpected the response, the more likely that laughter will follow.

When a good-looking young man named Art went to work at a New York newspaper, he was observed by two women from the editorial staff as he entered and left an elevator. "Who was that?" asked one woman admiringly. "Oh, that's Art," the other replied. "I know," said the first with a sly smile, "but what's his name?"

DOUBLE TAKES

"Slow Pedestrian Activity." (This sign would better describe all pedestrians, not just slow ones, by inserting a dash or colon after *Slow*.)

"Escape Calvin Klein." (The announcement of the new perfume needs some similar punctuation — or perhaps the word *by* before the man's name — unless the consumer hopes to escape Calvin Klein.)

"Woman Accused of Running Down Boyfriend Under Psychiatric Care." (This headline probably states the opposite of its intention; the woman, not the boyfriend, may need psychiatric care.)

"Dog Led Us to Murder Victims." (This macabre headline suggests the need to watch the two senses of *murder,* as noun and verb.)

"You have no idea how sorry I am." (This apology needs to be reworked unless the speaker wants to appear insincere.)

"Employers would be lucky to get this applicant to work for them." (A backhanded compliment, this line may cover a reluctance to recommend the applicant.)

"You have to see it to believe it!" (Here is a poor review for a show the reviewer apparently enjoyed; again, watch the possible misinterpretation.)

"Vicious Dog Owner Goes to City Jail." (Another headline; which one is vicious — the dog or the owner?)

"Special Children's Discount." (All children are special; this promotion should place *Children's* before *Special.*)

"Criminal Defense Attorney." (This job title appears to slander the jobholder; watch *criminal* as a modifier.)

"New Store Hours." (If the store is new, the sign should read "New Store's Hours"; if the hours are new, "Store's New Hours.")

"I've never seen anything like it!" (Another undercutting review for a film, this statement fails to suggest anything positive.)

"You won't believe our rates." (A hotel with this commercial is asking for customer disbelief; at the very least, *low* should be inserted before *rates.*)

"Our trucks have never run better." (This vehicle promotion should be stopped; what exactly does this ad say about the trucks offered previously?)

"I'm from Maryland. Ask me about the senator." (As a campaign slogan for a candidate seeking reelection, this wording can be taken as either for or against the candidate.)

"Keep out of reach of children." (This saying on medicine bottles sounds like advice from W. C. Fields; in shorthand wording, *product* should be specified after *Keep*.)

"Specials on Shirts $20 and Much More." (The store sporting this advertisement should think twice about using *much* for *many* — unless there are not "many more" specials and there is only "much more" cost.)

"There's no way you can be any better." (This apparent rave for an acting student leaves a sizable question mark about the speaker's genuine opinion.)

"Nothing tastes quite like our breakfast." (As a boast, this restaurant ad may well be taken the wrong way.)

"*Little Women* is the best reviewed movie of the year." (This promotion overlooks the possibility of well-written pans.)

10

EDITING

A SHORT-TERM DIET

ABRAHAM LINCOLN WAS still a lawyer when he was asked for his opinion of another member of the profession. His evaluation is telling: "He can compress the most words into the smallest idea of any man I ever met."

Verbal skills take work. First is the process of wording, followed by rewording, and then the hard part: editing. Wordiness and redundancy work together to slow communication, and the ability to recognize what is not needed and to remove it marks the power writer and speaker. Anything said right the first time should not need to be said again. Following that rule, however, seems nearly impossible for many word users, whose excessive redundancy yields powerless language.

Clocks appear "circular in shape," bicycles may be "blue in color," and days are "twenty-four hours in time" to careless word users. Drop the *in* phrase from each of those descriptions, and the effect will prove immediately stronger. Reworking words is the skill brought to bear by an editor, and every good writer and speaker can benefit from it.

WATCH FOR WORDINESS

"Mail your order today," a catalogue advises, "and receive a complimentary free gift." Redundancy runs rampant here. A gift costs the receiver nothing, so it should not be a "free gift" or, even worse, a "complimentary free gift."

Needless words lead to a lack of power. Business and government language is especially burdened by these unnecessary words and expressions, but almost any use of language will benefit from pruning and careful cutting.

One temptation may be to edit too much. Two centuries ago, Samuel Johnson repeated the advice of an old college tutor: "Read over your compositions, and wherever you meet with a passage which you think is particularly fine, strike it out." That approach may take editing a little too far, but the reader or speaker should at least beware wordiness.

To avoid wordiness, test words for their fitness. If the expression adds nothing to the meaning, feel free to remove it without causing a problem to the prose. According to some estimates, at least twenty-five percent of words add nothing to the language of business and may be excised immediately.

REVISE LAZY LANGUAGE

Some expressions take power away without adding anything to the message. These lackluster terms need to be kept to a minimum in power language. A number of them — *as it were* and *so to speak* and *to be sure* — carry little or no meaning in themselves; they fill space and make it harder for the audience to appreciate the needed words.

Up to leads off many a meaningless message. "The average commercial break can last up to four minutes," a report on television states, but the use of *up to* dilutes the data. Either try "A commercial break can last up to four minutes" or give specific information, as in "The average commercial break lasts a minute."

Some expressions are more awkward than they are wordy. "Astronomy is when somebody studies the stars and outer space" shows the awkward *is when* form in action. Save *is when* and *is where* specifically for statements about time and place. Also faulty is the phrase *is because,* often used redundantly in "the reason is because."

Other awkward expressions can be caught by realizing that a series of words adds nothing to the meaning. One speaker had already gone on too long when she said, "Just to sum it up in a true statement." Any sentence following that introduction should not need those words to begin unless the speaker has been lying up to that point. Remember the following five phrases and their instant, powerful replacements:

at this point in time = now
affected in a negative way = hurt
fail to tell the truth = lie
in view of the fact that = because
the present writer = I

Separate the filler from the forceful, and lackluster phrases will take on a shine that allows the audience to catch the message without the clutter.

REDO REDUNDANCY

Advertisers like to state and restate their message as much as possible. Some of their repetition, though, crosses the line into redundancy. A computer company announces, "Man has an increasing appetite for more and more speed," wasting the words *more and more* in the same sentence with *increasing.* A contest offers "a round-trip ticket to Europe and back."

Without that return, of course, the trip would fail to be a *round trip.*

"Let me once again reiterate," the public speaker thunders, and the audience, which needs only *reiterate,* may well be shuddering about too many words in an unnecessarily long speech. A publisher comments on "the many additions that are being added to the new directory," and readers may question why additions *are being added.*

Checking words for extra weight is one way to change prose from fat to fit. Word watchers may find that any number of expressions take more words than they are worth, and some examples have found their way into English as idioms (*the reason why* and *the place where* are especially overused), but the user of power language moves against this growing tide by delivering lean and clean phrases that carry the meaning.

"The most valuable of all talents," Thomas Jefferson once commented, "is that of never using two words when one will do."

One word is often plenty, especially one with the re- prefix. A newspaper report states, "This bustling entertainment zone will revert back to a quiet neighborhood next year," with *back* adding nothing to *revert.* The same holds true for "refer back," "return back," and even "retrace back."

When words are tied unnecessarily, as in the redundant "true facts," meaning becomes monotonous. Weak sentences begin with "The reason is because" or "The fact that." Legal pairs of words — "cease and desist" or "devise and bequeath" — may offer necessary shadings of meaning, but they are often repetitious. Certainly "working mother" is redundant.

Although every sentence may contain some unnecessary language, some examples of wordiness are more evident — and therefore more harmful — than others. Consider the lax language in the sentences below, and see which words can come out without a change in the meaning.

REDUNDANCIES

"Reserve your holiday order in advance." (*In advance* is the only time something can be reserved. The same is true of "advance appointment.")

"Every so often, take a brief respite from your work." (Any respite longer than *brief* becomes a vacation.)

"The candidate has been reticent to speak out." (*Reticence* is the reluctance *to speak out.*)

"It's a birthday surprise he was not expecting." (A *surprise* is always something the person is *not expecting.*)

"Jury Panel Paints Self-Portraits of Themselves." (This headline suggests that self-portraits can depict any subjects other than *themselves.*)

"Kills bugs dead." (This advertising slogan for insecticide is an example of verbal overkill.)

"I told him, I said, I'm not going." (Telling him is enough; *I said* adds nothing new.)

"The team set several new records last weekend." (A *record* is a record; there is nothing *new* about it.)

"Call now, and save fifty percent off the price." (Save words by using *save fifty percent* and dropping *off the price.*)

"There are lots of things that you and I share together." (One cannot *share separately.*)

"He's acting like a crazed lunatic." (Lunatics are crazed by definition.)

"We often attended the Saturday evening soirees." (Related to the French *soir* for "evening," the noun *soirees* can be held at no other time of day.)

"Their extra practice this week will obviate the need for more rehearsal this weekend." (There is no need for *the need for* with *obviate.*)

"It makes sense to visually see and audibly hear." (*See* and *hear* are enough without the redundant adverbs to split the infinitives.)

"Based on past experience, they figured about two thousand kids would show up." (*Experience* comes only from the *past*.)

"He was her former ex-boyfriend." (This doubled sense of past suggests that he is her current boyfriend; use either *ex-* or *former,* not both.)

"She frequented the restaurant quite often." (Without visiting *quite often,* a person cannot be said to *frequent* any specific place.)

"The landlord promised to make repairs to the hot water heater." (A water *heater* does not need *hot* to describe its purpose.)

"They entered the so-called 'black hole.'" (If something is *so-called,* it needs no set of quotation marks to set it off even more.)

"Prepare for a radical major change." (The first change should be to eliminate either *radical* or *major* from the sentence.)

"The new version was more distincter than the old." (The comparative *-er* suffix should be dropped when *more* is used.)

"Part of the border is formed by the Rio Grande River." (The Spanish *rio* means "river," which should not be repeated after *Rio Grande.*)

"This year's study will focus on the Sahara Desert." (*Sahara* is Arabic for "deserts"; remove the final word to avoid "Deserts Desert.")

"After remodeling, the end result will be an attractive and efficient airport." (Results come at the conclusion; leave off *end.*)

"The managers all shrugged their shoulders about the report." (Only shoulders can be shrugged, so *their shoulders* may be removed.)

"Off of the top of my head, I cannot cite the statistics." (*Off* and *of* come from the same root and should not be used together; drop *of.*)

"Advertisers aimed the product at the hoi polloi." (The Greek term *hoi polloi* means "the many," and *the* should never be used before it.)

"Remember the old adage about the early bird and the worm." (Every adage is *old,* making just *adage* enough.)

11

SENTENCES

CLAUSE AND EFFECT

A SENTENCE DOES NOT need to be long to express volumes. Consider the ancient inscription at Delphi: "Know thyself." The idea behind those two words has filled many a shelf of self-help books.

Although phrases may decorate a sentence, the sentence itself must include at least one clause, and the care that is taken with word selection for a phrase is even more urgent for a clause. The major subject-verb connection of a sentence is the main or independent clause, with dependent clauses less essential but still important to the structure.

A clause, a legal term for a part of a contract, proves equally enforceable in power language. The weaker the clause, the poorer the communication of the message will be.

SHAPE SENTENCES FORCEFULLY

"Be Cool in School!" exclaimed a poster in a fast-food restaurant. "Good Grades Has Its Rewards." The English of that sign earns a failing grade.

No matter how loose the rules of grammar have become, simple agreement of subject and verb must still be followed, as well as agreement in number of pronoun and antecedent. "Good Grades Have Their Rewards," a declarative sentence, is a passing version of the same sign.

The declarative mood marks the majority of sentences written and spoken. This mood communicates information and explains detail in the most direct way. The subject and the verb work together to express the idea of a declarative sentence. A main or independent clause may stand by itself as a sentence; a dependent or subordinate clause standing by itself ("When pigs fly") is a sentence fragment.

Standard sentences come in four forms:

1. Simple (subject and verb and object as needed): "I quit my job."
2. Compound (main clause and conjunction and main clause): "My daughter won the lottery, and I quit my job."
3. Complex (dependent clause and main clause): "When my daughter won the lottery, I quit my job."
4. Compound-Complex (complex sentence and conjunction and main clause): "When my daughter won the lottery, I quit my job, and I don't regret it." Remember to punctuate properly between sentences to avoid a run-on ("I quit my job I don't regret it") or a comma splice ("I quit my job, I don't regret it"). Use a conjunction or a semicolon between the independent clauses, or separate the two sentences with a period.

One trap with the declarative sentence is the urge to include far more information than is necessary. Avoid adding facts to the basic sentence if there is no need for them. In many cases, the sentence can be cut to its simplest form without harming the communication. If the added information seems important enough, perhaps another sentence is in order.

Some commercials are now being pitched without subjects

or helping verbs for their clauses: "Seen it! Been there! Done that!" These sentences stand out but also tend to leave the audience feeling incomplete, waiting for the right words. Emphasis may be overused with sentences that lack words and take exclamation points. "Warehouse jammed!" says a furniture company. "Stores full!" Other advertisers also drop verbs, although the billboard for a North Carolina hotel ("New Owner — Clean Rooms") may suggest that boarders will be expected to provide maid service.

Another clause trick is the reversal of standard syntax, placing the subject after the verb: "Leaving the building were the leaders of the summit." This technique, forceful if used occasionally, becomes too easily a habit and is best used rarely. The critic Wolcott Gibbs parodied this habit in magazines: "Backward ran sentences until reeled the mind."

SHARPEN SENTENCES POINTEDLY

"Witnesseth that for and in consideration of the covenants and conditions herein contained on the part of the lessee to be observed as performed, the lessor does hereby lease, let, and devise a building in its lot situate on the east side of Main Street upon the following terms and conditions." This language is a legal nightmare, one clause of a multipage contract drawn for leasing a small store. People disappear into the phrases "party of the first part" and "party of the second part," never to return as individuals. In an effort to cover everything, legal lingo loses its power quickly.

At the same time, denying reality is no more forceful. A real estate agent advertises: "I don't sell houses. I sell dreams." In fact, the agent sells houses first and then perhaps dreams; refusing to acknowledge the obvious makes the sentences seem weak or the speaker appear to be in denial.

With practice in editing, the seasoned writer or speaker

knows which material fulfills the purpose and which merely fills the space. At a second class meeting, the teacher said, "After ascertaining our former position, we should advance proportionately in covering the subsequent material." When the class stared back in disbelief, the teacher put the same sentence into plain English: "Let's move on." If in doubt, mark the sentence for subject and verb, seeing how much extra information has been included beyond the skeleton of the main clause. Sifting through that extra material may yield ideas for further sentences or content that may be cut to leave the audience content.

In many cases, a long and wordy clause may seem like a life sentence. The columnist James J. Kilpatrick criticized a *New York Times* sentence that separated subject and verb by twenty-three words. "The trouble with that sentence," he wrote, "is that the subject was in Wyoming and the verb was in New Jersey." Try to keep subject and verb tightly paired for power.

Perhaps the best way to sharpen clauses is to decide on the main point of the sentence and make sure it is found in the main clause. Other parts of the sentence may be dismissed as decoration, but the primary message should be positioned to be understood as the most significant part.

Recognizing a weak clause is not difficult. Usually the message is either missing or misplaced, forcing the audience to do the work for the word user.

VARY SENTENCES EFFECTIVELY

Obviously, not every clause can be whittled down to subject and verb without compromising the quality of the writing. A good rule for the placement of clauses calls for no more than two long clauses in a row. After the second long clause, the most effective sentence will be a short clause, especially if it contains the main idea of the passage.

The imperative mood, which issues commands and merely

implies its subject, should be used infrequently in writing and speaking. Listeners rarely respond to a series of orders any more than readers need to know the writer's every thought. This mood, however, can be effectively used, especially when combined with declarative sentences. After a series of declarative clauses, in fact, the imperative will stand out as advice to the audience. Take care not to overuse it, but in the right place, it can be most effective (note the imperative *take care* that starts this sentence).

Combining moods can work wonders. This technique is most effective when a short declarative sentence is followed by an even shorter imperative. "Knowledge is power," an actress confides. "Get some!" Even the advertising for a show — "The concert is Sunday. Be there!" — can take advantage of this technique.

Too many short clauses can be equally destructive, though, and the primary escape from this trap requires combining sentences. Note how a series of short sentences can be jarring: "The sun beat down. The heat was intense. It made the hikers panic." Instead, pull the sentences together to yield a combined force that the individual parts sorely lacked: "As the sun beat down, the intense heat made the hikers panic." The one longer sentence takes the place of the three short sentences, and the audience does less work to understand it. A health report complained: "The water is polluted. That is the problem." Watch how force can be added by combining the two clauses into one: "The problem is polluted water."

At the opposite extreme are mile-long sentences, literary if by Faulkner, faulty if by other writers. Some editors recommend a "standing on the bus" school of editing: the writer should picture the readers standing on a crowded bus. The same holds true for those long parenthetical comments that keep the reader from finding the simple subject and verb of a sentence. The less effective the prose, the more effort there is for the audience.

A phrase or clause may be inserted to help the audience. In the Gettysburg Address, Lincoln added a phrase — *on this continent* — between *brought forth* and *a new nation* to draw in the listeners. Humorists have a special knack for adding short clauses to supply crucial information or to point the way to a punch line. Dave Barry writes in his syndicated column, "The problem with winter sports is that — follow me closely here — they generally take place in winter." The writer Judith Viorst also knows just when to insert a subordinate clause for maximum effect. Watch the comic timing of her clause *when they read my poem* in the following book jacket note: "Judith Viorst says that she has been writing always — 'or at least since I was seven or eight, when I composed an ode to my dead parents, both of whom were alive and well and, *when they read my poem*, extremely annoyed.'"

The break for an inserted clause should come at a natural point, where somebody reading aloud may pause for breath. Otherwise, the interruption may seem stilted and bothersome.

Combining words and phrases into more forceful clauses can be effective for the message, but not when the combination makes no sense or sounds funny. The humorist Jean Kerr once reported a soap opera's dialogue that had startled her: "If I do have this baby," a woman threatened her husband, "it'll be on your head."

The final test of forceful clauses is whether the message says anything. Take the expression used and overused for years to end stories about a party or celebration: "A good time was had by all." To make sure the audience has a good time, sidestep the obvious and find fresh wording, perhaps by using a metaphor or other figure of speech.

A single metaphor can be a powerful thing. Consider this headline in *Variety* about the closing of the play *Angels in America:* "Costs Clip 'Angels' Wings." Word users often err when trying to extend the metaphor or when combining two metaphors accidentally into one; metaphorical mistakes will hurt the message (many also fall into the pit of clichés) and perhaps even embarrass the word user.

MIXED METAPHORS

"That's just gravy on the cake." (Cake tastes terrible with gravy on it; it's "That's pure gravy" or "That's just icing on the cake.")

"This much should hold me over for a little while." (Avoid *hold me over;* use *hold me for a little while* or *tide me over.*)

"Your excuses are not going to cut the muster." (*Mustard,* not *muster,* may be cut.)

"Her case somehow fell between the cracks." (Anything that falls *between the cracks* misses the cracks and hits a solid surface; try *through the cracks* or the British *between two stools.*)

"That's a whole new ball of worms." (The usual *can of worms* becomes entangled here with *ball of wax;* separate the metaphors.)

"We do have some light at the end of the horizon." (This statement by a weather forecaster mixes *on the horizon* with *at the end of the tunnel.*)

"They found themselves on the heels of a dilemma." (A dilemma is said to have two *horns,* not *heels,* which are usually reserved for the ancient cliché of *Achilles' heel.*)

"I think the detective must have some kind of sixth scent for tracking people." (A special power is a sixth *sense,* not to be confused with the bloodhound's *scent.*)

"He's tired of having to work like a banshee seven days a week." (Unless an actor is playing a banshee — a mournful Irish spirit — the correct similes are *work like a beaver* and *wail like a banshee.*)

"The company will be in dire straights if the policy isn't changed." (Navigating a boat through *dire straits* is the correct word picture.)

"As a comedian, he tries to keep up with his partner tongue and jowl." (Wry or ironic humor is called *tongue in cheek,* here apparently combined with the expression *cheek by jowl.*)

"Those people have been living in ivy-halled towers." (The *ivory tower* becomes overgrown with *halls of ivy,* a term for the academic world.)

"He was caught between a rock and the deep blue sea." (The sense of predicament may be expressed as *between a rock and a hard place* or *between the devil and the deep blue sea.*)

"The police suggested seeking a cease and disorder." (Here the *seek and desist order* is mixed up with *disorderly conduct.*)

"Those two are the glue that ties everything together." (Glue cannot tie; either *rope that ties* or *glue that holds* makes a better metaphor.)

"That guy doesn't even know which road to hoe." (The farming metaphor is *row to hoe,* combined here with *road to take.*)

"Marrying him was an escape goat for her." (Watch out for the different terms *scapegoat* and *escape route.*)

"The sailors were told to tow the line from now on." (Here *toe the line* seems to be tangled with *tow a rope.*)

12

SYNTAX

IN WORKING ORDER

"I LIVE FOR syntax," Raymond Chandler once said, with more than a little hyperbole detected.

A question is repeated thousands of times every day in government and business offices across the country: "What can I do you for?" The word order, or syntax, of that question sounds strange, but its widespread use suggests a playfulness with the language not found in its normal word order ("What can I do for you?"). Knowing when to use good syntax and when to play with it is an important skill of power language.

Syntax makes a difference not only in short phrases but also in long clauses, forcing the skillful word user to be aware of where the sentence started and how it progresses. Losing control of the syntax destroys the message and confuses the communication. The ability to track syntax and keep the words flowing becomes second nature to the user of power language.

PUT WORDS INTO PROPER ORDER

When words move out of their proper order, humor may ensue. *Variety* awarded the Press Release of the Year award in 1994 to a station that advertised its lead show "is heading into the May sweeps with a full steam of head." Similarly, Kentucky Fried Chicken offers "a whole Colonel's rotisserie chicken," prompting the misreading of "a whole Colonel" rather than "a whole chicken."

The poet Samuel Taylor Coleridge once commented that prose is "words in the best order" and poetry "the best words in the best order." The use of *best* implies a single way to order words, but even the fledgling writer or speaker can find numerous ways to say the same thing. Trying the different methods may well produce a *best* way to word, and working with words provides experience in producing better and stronger language.

Not working carefully with words, on the other hand, may be a sure approach to disaster, causing a random order that obscures the message and disturbs the audience. A *TV Guide* summary insists, "On the way to the airport to catch a flight to the islands, heavy snow maroons the family"; snow, however, rarely catches a flight to the islands. If not the *best* order, at least a working order is needed to keep the ideas flowing in a sensible pattern.

Three errors are most likely to damage word ordering. First is the misplaced modifier; a commercial presents "the law firm that has represented victims since 1980," but *since 1980* should follow *that*, not *victims*. Second is the dangling modifier, which has no subject to describe: "Getting soaked, the rain caused problems" has no one to receive the soaking. The third form is the squinting modifier, which causes the correct reading to remain unclear: a medical report argues, "Drinking often causes problems," which may be read either as "drinking often" or as "often causes problems." Similarly squinting is *too much* in

"He likes to eat too much," because either the servings or the enjoyment may be excessive.

BUILD TO THE MOST FORCEFUL WORDS

"From where the sun now stands," said Chief Joseph of the Nez Percé, "I will fight no more forever." The *forever* that ended the chief's surrender to the U.S. Army in 1877 gains all the more power from its position at the end of the sentence. Concluding words linger longest, and the strongest speakers know the value of this key. Memorable terms should be saved for that final position, the last word to be left with the reader or listener.

Words should build in strength. Taking too much medication, several experts warned in a medical advisory, can be "deadly and dangerous." Note how the phrase falls off because the stronger term comes first. If something is deadly, by definition it is dangerous, but not every dangerous thing is also deadly. Build up to the most powerful term, leading the audience to a new height rather than a letdown.

Arrange lists of words to keep the reader or listener in suspense. Expending the most powerful word first in a sentence causes what follows to suffer, failing to bolster the argument or the explanation. A defiant character on a television drama, when warned not to go somewhere, announces, "I will and I can"; ability *(can)* is weaker than resolution *(will)*, making "I can and I will" a stronger order. "We'll travel everywhere," promises a children's show, "from out of this world to around the block." That statement puts the extraordinary *(out of this world)* before the mundane *(around the block)*, again pulling the punch of the prose.

Sometimes building order may be reversed, placing the stronger idea first. In those cases, however, the second idea is usually discounted by using *just* or *only*. For instance, reverse order works in the Carole King song "Will You Love Me Tomorrow?": the plaintive singer asks whether the pleasure is permanent or *just* temporary.

In ordering words, however, do not separate the main subject and verb with a long list of phrases or modifiers. The main action of the sentence should always be clear. In the same way, a direct object should never be distant from its verb: "He threw, with all his might to a player in left field, the baseball." Also, do not force unrelated information into the sentence in a hopeless non sequitur: "Born in Arkansas, the president proposed additional funding for the Pacific project."

Weigh each word in the list to determine its force, and arrange the words from least powerful to most forceful. Think of the words as individual steps, leading to the highest point as the audience is led along.

QUALIFY WITH CARE

Watch out for *only,* perhaps the single most misplaced word in the English language. Consider the statement "Pollution hurts people" and the various places that "only" can be inserted. "Only pollution hurts people" suggests that weapons and other harmful things do not exist. "Pollution only hurts people" indicates that pollution cannot kill, although it certainly can. "Pollution hurts only people" denies the reality of the deadly effects on plant and animal life. The placement of *only* can make all the difference to the message being conveyed.

In *Northanger Abbey* in 1818, the novelist Jane Austen took umbrage at the short word, especially in the denigrating phrase "only a novel." After hearing that putdown, she wrote her definition of "only a novel": "Or, in short, only some work in which the most thorough knowledge of human nature, the happiest delineation of its varieties, the liveliest effusions of wit and humor are conveyed to the world in the best chosen language."

Only, of course, is not the only such word. Watch out also for *just* and *even* and *merely,* qualifiers that limit but must be used to limit the proper quantity. *Also* is also dangerous and best placed carefully.

That is sometimes a restricter, and its placement or omission can make a big difference. "She told him she was leaving" means the same as "She told him that she was leaving." A moment of misreading is possible, though, when something that looks like a direct object follows: "She revealed her intention was to leave" may be misunderstood as "She revealed her intention," a misreading eliminated by inserting *that:* "She revealed that her intention was to leave."

Even the time elements must be placed carefully. "He said yesterday that he would leave" does not mean the same thing as "He said that he would leave yesterday," which puts a more specific time on his leaving. "A *famous* list of directors" and "a *hot* cup of coffee" are also examples of words out of order, especially when it is the directors who are famous and the coffee that is hot.

The danger in placing qualifiers correctly can be the violation of idiom. "All is not lost," for example, indicates that nothing is missing, whereas "Not all is lost" suggests that at least something has been lost. The placement of *not* can change the meaning, although not everybody understands this difference.

CONSIDER OTHER WORDING POSSIBILITIES

Sometimes the order of words makes little difference. A General Motors advertisement explains that "common chemicals in the air are causing rust in every part of America." Moving "in every part of America" to the front of that sentence does not improve the bad news.

Other times, the order leads to sentences that sound strange. A morning talk show guest says, "They are taken very well care of," and the syntax alarm goes off. "They are very well taken

care of" and "They are taken care of very well" are two possibilities that should have been considered.

Try to keep words in conversational order as often as possible.
"She today announced the winner" will never have the conversational quality of "She announced the winner today" or "Today she announced the winner."

A trick of sentencing places the strongest word at the start or
the finish. Modifiers, though, should always come close to the
word being described, and that word must always appear in the
sentence. "Six feet tall, his hair was bright red" suggests long,
long hair.

In assembling a sentence, the writer or speaker needs to be
aware that the parts carry a built-in logic, one that is defied
by careless construction. Looking over the possibilities before
choosing the final wording will help break the illogical patterns
and make the sentence more comprehensible.

Syntax may be varied to catch the audience's attention. "Here
comes the — no, that's not him" is an example of anacoluthon,
a shift in midsentence to surprise or catch offguard. Anas-
trophe, or reversing normal sentence order, also does the trick:
"Out you go" or "Here am I."

Placing the adjective after the noun it modifies can also be ef-
fective. From time immemorial, poets have been turning word
order around, from Poe's "Once upon a midnight dreary" to the
Christmas hymn "We Three Kings of Orient Are," and Henry
Wadsworth Longfellow began the epic poem *Evangeline* with
"This is the forest primeval."

Watch where the words fall and fail in the sentences that
follow. After each example, the problem words are pointed toward their proper order to give each sentence a solid syntax.
Notice that some modifiers are dangling — they have nothing
in the sentence to modify. Sometimes comic phrases result:
"The bullet is in her yet" led one woman to ask what part of the
body is a *yet*.

Groucho Marx made a comic career out of word disorder.

Perhaps his best is "One morning I shot an elephant in my pajamas. How he got in my pajamas, I'll never know!"

OUT OF ORDER

"At age two, his parents became missionaries and relocated to South Africa." (An amazing achievement for two-year-olds, this sentence seems to suggest; instead, the phrase *at age two* dangles because it has no *he* to modify.)

"We have some ideas in our minds that are not quite right." (Unless the minds are fading, *that are not quite right* belongs next to *ideas*.)

"I have the money from the bank in my wallet." (Few wallets come with banks inside them; try "The money from the bank is in my wallet.")

"This drama is a pep talk for middle-age women masquerading as a play." (The women are not *masquerading as a play*; move that phrase closer to *pep talk*.)

"The cow is an animal with an udder that goes 'moo.'" (Farmers will point out that it is not the udder that goes *moo*; substitute "animal that has an udder and goes 'moo.'")

"He accepted an honorary Oscar for lifetime achievement from a hospital bed." (This unlikely category for an award — "lifetime achievement from a hospital bed" — would be better expressed by placing "from a hospital bed" at the start of the sentence.)

"It's like the man who lost a bet on a ball game with a guy at work." (If the ball game is not being played "with a guy at work," then that expression should follow *bet*.)

"As a former member, we know you are interested in art." (The former member is probably *you*, not *we*; move "as a former member" next to *you*.)

"Guests will dine on veal stuffed with sweetbreads from the chef." (This grotesque image can be reworked by changing *from* to *prepared by*.)

"He was pronounced dead as a result of massive head injuries by the coroner." (Unless the police have arrested the coroner, "by the coroner" should appear after "pronounced dead.")

"I put out the garbage at night instead of him." (To make clear that the garbage is being put out by a different person, move "instead of him" to the start of the sentence.)

"Visiting Great Britain, the queen invited the first lady to tea." (The queen lives in Great Britain; to clarify the sentence, place *visiting Great Britain* after *the first lady.*)

"As foreigners living in a largely overcrowded neighborhood, our garbage is collected irregularly." (Garbage is not *foreigners*; this dangling modifier needs *we find that* inserted after the comma.)

"I'm going to marry a wonderful man in a wonderful dress." (This sentiment paints the wrong word picture; move *in a wonderful dress* to the beginning.)

"The story was discovered after the writer's death in a desk drawer." (The writer was not found in the desk drawer; try that final phrase after *discovered.*)

"She was given an animal by a New Jersey farmer that she intends to donate to the zoo." (Zoos will not accept farmers; rework the start of the sentence as "A New Jersey farmer gave her an animal that.")

"Our panel will offer a free discussion of civil rights on Tuesday." (Every day should have civil rights; place *on Tuesday* at the start.)

"Others in France have their music still." (Unless the music is silent, move *still* to follow *France.*)

13

TRANSITIONS

POWER CONNECTIONS

SOMETIMES THE SHORTEST words make the biggest difference. *And* puts together; *or* separates; *but* contradicts. Transitions are just as important as conjunctions, and the experts in this field include news broadcasters and game show hosts, who use them frequently. When a contestant on a game show commented that the experience "had been rewarding," the host immediately added, "And this round you've been rewarded with . . ." Television reporters are even more abrupt with their transitions, often finishing their report by saying the name of the news anchor as if it were a question: "And that's the news from Los Angeles. Dan?"

Without the right connections, words often fall into nonsensical patterns, misleading the audience. Beware the *non sequitur*, Latin for "it does not follow." The weakest way to put words together is to ignore the connections built into the language, following one idea with another thought apparently unrelated to the first.

Try to envision the language as a stream, a continuous flow that moves gently from one point to the next without noticeable interruption. Just as word order should be set up as helpfully as steppingstones across a river, transitions and conjunctions show the way from one step to the next. Leaving out the connecting word may leave the audience stranded in midstream.

Sometimes the lack of connection is between paragraphs or sentences. Transitions can make the connection clear. Even in the same sentence, however, any noticeable non sequitur will prove jarring to the reader or hearer and stop the natural flow of language.

LINK IDEAS MEANINGFULLY

Some usage experts forbid starting a sentence with a conjunction such as *and* or *but*. Worse, however, is the failure to provide any conjunction to link the ideas being offered. In a first draft, sentences may be jotted down without that connection, but rewriting requires the use of linking words.

Once a conjunction has been chosen, be careful not to overwork it. If a paragraph already contains *but*, avoid any additional contradictions in the same paragraph. With both *but* and *however* in the same paragraph, for instance, each sentence begins to contradict what went before, and the audience is left groundless.

Find ways to smooth the way for readers and listeners, and the argument will be rewarded with extra power. A choppy explanation, full of unrelated ideas, may dissuade the audience; contrarily, a flowing argument helps move the audience past even the weakest points to the strongest evidence.

Listen to the conjunctions at work in the poetry of William Butler Yeats: "When you are old and gray and full of sleep, / And nodding by the fire. . . ." Adding every detail with *and* lulls the reader along. Short, sharp sentences would produce the opposite effect.

CONNECT WITH THE CORRECT CONJUNCTION

The power of conjunctions rests in their proper use. *And* suggests an equal linking, while *but* provides opposition (this sentence is the rare kind that even language purists will agree may start with *and*). The more sophisticated conjunctions, from *however* to *nevertheless,* require careful handling to make sure their negative spin holds true. When one idea flows from another, *however* is a mistake.

Other conjunction mistakes depend on the formality of the writing. Too many formal discourses have come to accept the jocular *plus* from advertising as a legitimate conjunction for linking serious ideas. Save *plus* for conversation, and replace it in formal discourse with the simpler *and.* In addition, symbols should not be used; stay away from the *plus* sign (+) and the ampersand (&).

Finally, pair conjunctions correctly. *Neither* should lead to *nor,* just as *either* promises *or.* The list may be long ("Neither rain nor hail nor sleet nor dark of night") or, as purists prefer, short ("neither here nor there").

ALSO, SMOOTH THE WAY WITH TRANSITIONS

Transitions, such as *also,* work the magic of conjunctions on longer passages. From one sentence to the next within a paragraph, transitions may not seem necessary. Once the paragraph ends and another begins, however, some way must be offered to connect their ideas.

For example, the prepositional phrase *for example* leads from a general discussion to a specific case. Overused, perhaps, for the start of a different approach is *on the other hand,* most disturbing when more than two possibilities are discussed. Save the right transition for the right moment, depending on which direction the argument is taking. Like good traffic signals, the right transitions not only take shape from what they follow but also point ahead to what to expect.

Not every transition has to be a set word *(also)* or an overused phrase *(in another case)*. An article that ends one paragraph with a mention of Edgar Allan Poe's poem *The Raven* begins the next paragraph with "Never more popular." The parroting of the raven's favorite expression, *nevermore,* connects the two paragraphs subtly yet forcefully. The writer or speaker should connect words as smoothly as possible, but the transitions may be as unexpected or surprising, when the work is done, as the information being presented.

No man is an island; no sentence is, either. Writers of fiction know how to move readers from sentence to sentence. A character described in one paragraph as "a plump middle-aged man" may be found in the next paragraph as "the plump man."

Without signals, accidents occur. A widely circulated list of insurance company reports has comments from policyholders trying to describe their accidents briefly. "My car was legally parked," said one driver, "as it backed into the other vehicle"; the illogic in that sentence would be fixed by using the conjunctive adverb *before* in place of *as.*

These traffic signs should never be taken for granted. In both writing and speaking, the transition or conjunction leads the way for the presentation of thoughts in a graceful, logical order. *So* is not an all-purpose connector; it makes no sense in the claim "The pedestrian had no idea which direction to go, so I ran over him." Instead, it should be used to lead from one idea to the next: "I took the job so that I could pay my bills."

Furthermore (another leading word), even the deliberate lack of conjunctions may provide force. Julius Caesar used no *and* in his three-part motto: "I came, I saw, I conquered." This technique, known as asyndeton, has as its counterpart the multiconjunction style known as polysyndeton. A flat listing of Christmas details, for instance, loses the cumulative and breathless power of the repeated conjunction in setting the scene of "the candles and the tree and the music and the stories and the laughter." Rossiter Raymond, a mining engineer and Sunday school teacher, used *and* efficiently to move the listeners of his World War I prayer: "Life is eternal; and love is immortal; and death is only a horizon; and a horizon is nothing save the limit of our sight."

Allow *and* to build the power of a sentence, being careful not to combine too much information for the sentence to be understood easily (one insurance claimant responded, "I had been driving my car for forty years when I fell asleep at the wheel and had an accident"). Remember, though, that many language authorities frown on using a conjunction such as *and* to begin a sentence; the user should be aware of the controversy before deciding to try that approach.

Other conjunction errors are clearer. The following sentences offer cases of mistaken conjunctions. Each of the examples is followed by an explanation of the correct conjunction.

BROKEN CONNECTIONS

"Neither the defense or the prosecution has seen the sworn declaration." (This line from a legal brief is too brief; the *or* should not be coupled with *neither*: "Neither the defense nor the prosecution. . . .")

"Both wrestlers competed for the title." (Here the connection is not a conjunction but the use of *both* as an adjective; the two wrestlers are competing, which makes *both* redundant: "The two wrestlers competed. . . .")

"Firstly, jurors are going to know the truth." (Lose the legalistic *firstly* — an error for *first* — which requires *secondly* and *thirdly* to follow; the sentence is stronger without the weak transition.)

"See this lavish but suspenseful adaptation of F. Scott Fitzgerald's Jazz Age classic." (This plug for *The Great Gatsby* suggests that *lavish* is opposed to *suspenseful;* use *and* instead to link these equal modifiers.)

"We have roots where others have branches." (The bank using this advertisement does not physically have roots *where* others have branches; the correct word is *while,* indicating "at the same time," not "at the same place.")

"Also yesterday morning, the traffic was bad." (This cluster of transitions may lead to a clogged transmission of the message; move *yesterday morning* to the end of the sentence.)

"Neither James, Jane, nor Robert will be able to attend." (The pairing of *neither . . . nor* fits better with two possibilities, not three or more; try "James, Jane, and Robert will not be able to attend.")

"Like I said, I do not approve of smoking in public." (Grammar purists will explain that *like* is a preposition, and *as* is the conjunction that leads into a subject and verb; substitute "As I said. . . .")

"I left early, but I must report, however, that I was deeply moved by the show." (Do not overdo the conjunctions; either *however* or *but* is enough contradiction for the sentence.)

"Do you have $200 you can spare? Either do I!" (This protest would be stronger with the correct word; the negative sense of *either* should be "Neither do I!")

"I can't help but worrying about you." (Sometimes a negative conjunction can be left out entirely; try the same sentence without the use of *but.*)

"This is not the time nor the place." (This sentence contains a double negative with *not* and *nor;* use either "neither the time nor the place" or "not the time or the place.")

14

TONE

TONING UP

"I COULD CARE LESS." These four words look innocuous, but the combination grates on many word watchers, and the principal flaw is one of tone. The words, a sarcastic version of "I couldn't care less," have moved from spoken to written English, but with no way to convey the tone of the spoken sarcasm. As a result, the writer seems to be saying the opposite of the intended message, and meaning trips over itself.

A speaker uses a physical voice; a writer's voice comes from within, a collection of chosen words and practiced ways of linking them. Sarcasm, which can work well in speaking, rarely finds its target in the written word; the writer runs the risk of having the reader take the words seriously. Much the same as the response to Orson Welles's infamous "invasion from Mars" broadcast, the results can be far different from what was expected. Finding the right voice is a necessary part of power language.

Problems with tone are easy to detect. A student writing an essay about Shakespeare comments on "the plays Bill wrote," and that informal tone fills the paper. Similarly, nobody who delivers a eulogy should try to make light of death, because lightness would be another wrong choice of tone.

"Don't use that tone with me!" an overwrought parent shouts at a child, the parent no longer in control of the tone or the situation. Finding the right tone marks the way to successful communication.

ALWAYS VALUE CONTENT OVER TONE

This rule is among the most important for power language. The user of powerful words never loses sight of the purpose in communicating and knows that content always counts more than tone. At no time should the writer or speaker be so caught up in conveying the message that the message itself suffers.

Knowing *what* is to be said should always take precedence over *how* it is said. A corporate report full of mirth and light anecdotes should not be used to mask the prospect of layoffs in the near future. A false tone, or a tone that overshadows content, leads to false expectations and later to claims of misleading language.

Marrying content and tone, however, is a major precept of power language. Once aware of the message and its intended audience, the writer or speaker should adopt the tone most appropriate for the communication. The world's power speakers have long known this rule and been recognized for their ability to wed wisdom and wit.

For many years, students were discouraged from using the pronouns *I* and *you* in their writing in favor of a dispassionate third-person point of view. Times are changing, and nowadays corporate reports are sometimes written in the first person. An occasional shift from one viewpoint to another can have a powerful effect. What should be avoided, however, is the hundred-word essay in which the pronoun *I* and its various other forms (*me, myself,* and *my*) appear twenty times. One in every five words should not be a self-reference, even in a vanity piece.

BE SINCERE

"What greater crime can an orator be charged with," asked Demosthenes in the greatest speech of ancient Greece, "than that his opinions and his language are not the same?" Sincerity matters. To be as sincere as possible, follow the guidance of Dr. Seuss's Horton the Elephant: "I meant what I said, and I said what I meant." If that much integrity is not possible, then at least aim for sincerity. An expert on dating says of pickup lines, "It doesn't matter what's said so long as it's sincere."

To convey words with power, the speaker or writer needs to strive for sincerity. Believing in the message gives an edge that no amount of preparation or rewording can match. "Be sincere," the press agent tells his client, a struggling actor. "If you can fake that, you've got it made."

Humility can be a forceful tone, even with a certain amount of fakery. When Mark Antony addresses the citizens of Rome after Julius Caesar's assassination, his words strike with extra force because he does not sound pompous or overbearing. Shakespeare gives him the repeated line "And these are all honorable men," with simply the changing tone of *honorable* as the key to his true intent. When Fidel Castro decided to stop smoking cigars, he did not say that deception was wrong. Instead, he told an interviewer for *Cigar Aficionado* magazine that he would not smoke secretly: "I wouldn't want three, four, or five people knowing that I was deceiving others."

Genuine concern shines through any attempt to put words together, and a candid admission can make the words even stronger. A young chef tells the *New York Times*, "More than half of my cuisine is the quality of the products," adding, "Only about forty percent is my work." Humility, the root of the Seven Virtues, pays off with its own quiet power.

Study the message to determine the level of concern it deserves, and try to convey that concern to the audience. Emotion may well be brought into play, but a controlled emotion allows the writer or speaker to take charge of the words, not to be driven by them.

When George Orwell wrote his influential essay "Politics and the English Language" in 1950, he recognized a growing crisis: "The great enemy of clear language is insincerity. When there is a gap between one's real and one's declared aims, one turns . . . to long words and exhausted idioms, like a cuttlefish squirting out ink." Strive for sincerity, if only to avoid being compared to a cuttlefish.

HELP THE AUDIENCE CARE

"You come too," Robert Frost writes, inviting readers into one of his poems. Every writer and speaker has a variety of tones and voices for reaching an audience. For power language to succeed, the word user must search out and recognize the appropriate tone for the message to be conveyed, making the audience feel welcome in the process.

Just as a eulogy requires a certain somberness, so every speaking and writing situation should be guided by the appropriate tone. Gauging that tone becomes the responsibility of the word user, who must determine the right level for the message, and a large part of recognizing the tone comes by knowing the audience as well as the purpose of the communication. A pink slip is no time for levity, nor is an anniversary card a time for anger. Mark the time by the tone, and the communication soars.

Directly addressing the audience can decide the tone. "Listen, my children," Longfellow begins his poem of Paul Revere's ride, and the audience is immediately gathered into the message. Choose the right term for the audience; business reports and student essays would lose power by referring to the audience as "my children," but the encompassing of the audience should somehow be expressed, much as Mark Antony gathers his listeners with "Friends, Romans, countrymen."

If the wording does not sound conversational, power will be

lost. Use the words that offer the most meaning. Often these words are the first that one thinks of and are then replaced with longer words for fear of seeming simplistic. *Proactive* adds nothing to *active.* The verb *redact* sounds more technical than *edit,* but it usually adds little more than the straightforward *cut* provides. Even *excessive returns* may make a business leader's day, but one leader tells his managers in conversational terms, "*Profit* is a great word."

To profit from power language, show confidence in the words chosen. That confidence should not be excessive, but neither should the speaker sabotage the words from the start. Eliminate such comments as "I know this isn't any good, but. . . ." Such an opening apology will downgrade whatever follows in the minds of the audience, and the speaker has nobody else to blame for that loss of power.

Reach beyond personal views as much as possible to hold people's attention. Many English teachers still frown on the use of *I,* largely because the emphasis on self keeps the audience from caring about the views expressed. Find what the other person wants to know about, and stick with that topic. An obsession about self needs a decisive change of topic, not the wavering of the egotist who says, "I've talked about myself enough. So what do you think of me?"

EDITORIALIZE WITH CAUTION

"He works for a corporation" states a fact, something that can be verified or denied. "He works for a corporation that has grown too big" moves from fact into opinion.

Persuading the audience often requires the use of words that connote good or evil, power or weakness. *Too big* is editorializing, a value judgment that cannot be proved or disproved. The ability to recognize these words allows the user of power language to understand the appropriate times for their use.

A newspaper article, for example, should remain as free of

bias as possible, without opinionated words to sway the reader. An editorial, by contrast, aims to move the reader to action or to influence the views of that reader, so value judgments are inevitable in editorials.

Consider the effects of emotional language before using any opinionated words in writing or speaking. Knowing when to push these words and when to pull back provides the word user with an effective system of controls.

In the sentences below, watch for editorializing in the tone of the words. The leader of a mob may be said by some to *inspire*, by others to *incite* (and *mob* itself is an editorializing word for a *crowd*). Each example is followed by less biased language, words that should be substituted when the aim is not to be emotional or unobjective.

EDITORIAL EYES

"The corporation was paid not more than a billion dollars." (*Not more than* makes a large amount sound small; aim for an exact figure.)

"He worked for the state press and served as a mouthpiece for the government." (The slang *mouthpiece* suggests control or manipulation; tone it down to *official spokesman*.)

"She maintains that all the money has been properly accounted for." (The verb *maintains* suggests that she may be lying; use the neutral *says*.)

"He has the support of all his cronies in the statehouse." (The noun *crony* implies not only age but also excessive influence; try *colleagues*.)

"The elected candidates took their rightful positions as the leaders." (*Rightful* implies a bias that the user should admit to or explain; it can easily be left out.)

"He insists that no extra expenses will be incurred." (Like *maintain*, the verb *insists* indicates disbelief; use *says*.)

"The amazing fact was repeated throughout the testimony."

(*Amazing* makes a judgment that needs to be supported, and few facts are worthy of such a strong description.)

"They failed to complete the project by the end of the month." (Perhaps they *chose* not to complete the project; the sense of failure or deliberate error may make *failed* inappropriate.)

"Two rival groups tried to take credit for the bombing." (No attack should be given *credit*; the word is *responsibility*.)

"Police were called in to handle the brutal attack on the protesters." (*Brutal* is a judgment that would perhaps be disputed by those who fought with the protesters; either delete the word or be able to support it with facts and details.)

III

POWER STRUCTURES

HOW TO BUILD WITH WORDS

15

BEGINNING

POWER STARTS

"I KNOW WHAT I want to say, but I can't seem to get started." Far less serious than writer's block, the blank page or first spoken word presents an obstacle that can be easily overcome. Even accomplished novelists have experienced this tension. "When I face the desolate impossibility of writing five hundred pages," John Steinbeck wrote in *Travels with Charley* in 1962, "a sick sense of failure falls on me and I know I can never do it. This happens every time. Then gradually I write one page and then another. One day's work is all I can permit myself to contemplate and I eliminate the possibility of ever finishing."

The selection of starting words should always make the audience want to hear more. A false start is any beginning that makes the audience long for the ending. Speakers often draw a laugh with "Before starting my speech today, there's something I want to say." Used without the intention of humor, however, lengthy prepositional phrases and dangling modifiers stupefy the reader or listener long before the main point has been made.

In the first place, do away with the word wasting of leads such as *In the first place.* Without the biblical solemnity of *In the beginning* or the rhetorical brevity of *First,* these four words warn of more wordiness to come and perhaps remind the audience of better places to be.

HAVE SOMETHING TO SAY

This key may sound obvious, but forgetting it may cause many speeches and papers to go astray. The word user must have a message to offer, and if necessary, must do the research to support the points being made. Without taking that time or making that effort, the writer or speaker will fail to gain the audience's interest or trust.

Anybody perpetually at a loss for something to say should recognize the need for more depth to his or her life, at least the life of the mind. Reading helps, but it alone does not promote power language. In the seventeenth century, Sir Francis Bacon recognized the three essential elements for well-rounded wording. "Reading maketh a full man," he wrote, "conference a ready man, and writing an exact man."

Every word user should consider that advice and aim for exactness in wording. The repeated use of "What I really mean to say" almost always signals the audience that what has gone before is a mistake, information to be ignored. Before writing or speaking, decide what the message will be and hold to that plan. Anything less may suggest that the word user has nothing meaningful to say.

START DELIBERATELY

A journalism teacher asked each of her thirty students to write a newspaper article based on the same list of facts. The stories would cover the increase in a local bakery's business over the past year. Twenty-nine of the completed articles started flatly with a statement of that increased business; the thirtieth began, "Yeast is raising a lot more dough this year."

Only the writer or speaker, knowing the message to be conveyed, can choose the most effective starting point for the message. Armed with that knowledge, however, the word user is free to aim for a power start. Following are the ten most powerful ways to set out, each a rhetorical device to overcome the anxiety of beginning:

1. Person: "Scarlett O'Hara was not beautiful" is the opening volley of *Gone With the Wind*, centering the story on its main character but without romanticizing her.
2. Place: "Way down upon the Swanee River" begins the Stephen Foster song, provoking memories of a familiar yet distant place.
3. Time: "Once upon a time" or, as Chaucer began *The Canterbury Tales* six hundred years ago, "Whan that Aprill with his shoures soote / The droghte of March hath perced to the roote."
4. Contradiction: "'No man is an island,' the poet John Donne wrote, but he obviously never met. . . ."
5. Controversy: "Lizzie Borden was framed."
6. Correction of a "fact": "The Mexican jumping bean, contrary to popular belief, is not a bean."
7. Question: "What happened to Amelia Earhart?"
8. Power phrase: "In the beginning" works twice in the Bible.
9. Inclusiveness: "We the people of the United States" makes the Constitution's start a shining example of political strength and unity.
10. Imperative mood: "Call me Ishmael" begins *Moby Dick*, and the reader is pulled into the narrative force of a character — who may or may not be giving his true name.

Even the weaker words *there* and *it* may be used to begin, as long as they are used deliberately. The beginning of a novel by Edward Bulwer-Lytton — "It was a dark and stormy night" — has been hopelessly parodied, but Charles Dickens used the pronoun to better effect in *A Tale of Two Cities* ("It was the best of times, it was the worst of times"). *There* can also lead off; in a musical example, Ethel Merman's powerhouse voice introduced the Irving Berlin song "There's No Business Like Show Business."

SHOW THE SCENE

Many speakers try to begin with a joke, just as many writers aim to use a quotation. In both cases, the most important job for the word user is to set the scene of that joke or quotation. Wrapping the humor or pointed words in a story allows the audience to visualize what may have attracted the writer to that anecdote or quotation and keeps the significant saying from being thrown away in a single sentence unrelated to the speech or writing as a whole.

"What is the question?" Gertrude Stein reportedly asked about life.

The quotation in itself is curious, perhaps even striking, but hardly so intriguing as when wrapped in the circumstances of its saying. Gertrude Stein was on her deathbed, reflecting on a long and sometimes difficult life and looking for answers to even more difficult questions. She asked, "What is the answer?" When no answer came, her last words were "In that case, what is the question?"

Now the quotation stands out and tells readers or listeners why they should care about those words rather than other phrases Stein may have used during her lifetime. Set the scene so that the audience can appreciate not only the starting words but also the message that follows the introduction.

OVERCOME FALSE STARTS

False starts abound in the efforts of writers and speakers. The faulty beginnings may be lengthy stories that have nothing to do with the topic at hand. More often, these starts are wordy phrases that lack imagination and tend to turn off rather than stimulate the imagination of the audience.

Unproductive words and empty phrases are the leading examples of false starts. Recognizing the lack of power in these terms should help the writer or speaker avoid bumpy beginnings that detract from the message and make winning over the audience that much harder. Audiences may well tune out any talk that starts with "Well, first of all." The words are unnecessary, threatening to take longer than necessary, and the speech has barely begun.

Also, citing a name is not enough. To write or speak about a specific person, begin with enough identification to breed familiarity with the audience. People such as Oprah Winfrey or Stephen King are widely known and hold specific images for the listener, so extra identification is often unnecessary (especially heavy-handed explanations such as "a well-known television personality" or "a best-selling horror novelist"). For lesser-known persons, identification may be needed, and it should be attached as closely as possible to the name. "Christina Rossetti, the nineteenth-century poet, wrote" sounds much more natural than "Christina Rossetti, in one of the nineteenth-century poems that made her famous."

A name alone is never enough. Find something unusual or noteworthy to discuss about the person. *Spin* is the term used by political analysts for promoting a certain angle of a news story, and powerful writing and speaking about a named person can also use some spin.

The name-first policy probably works best whenever the writing leads off with a quotation. Remember to let the reader or listener know immediately who is speaking; the name provides the first link in the chain of words. "Mark Twain once said" or "Erma Bombeck says" almost guarantees a rapt audience for whatever follows.

The opening comment often points the way for writers and speakers to continue. Consider Effie Perine, the selfless, devoted, twenty-four-hour-a-day secretary to Sam Spade in Dashiell Hammett's mysteries. The opening proposition of a debate or the theme for an essay may be "There are no Effie Perines anymore." At least three responses are possible:

1. "There never were. Effie is a fictional character, and I doubt that any real person would. . . ."
2. "Sure, there are. I know a secretary who is so devoted to her work that. . . ."
3. "Thank goodness! Effie Perine was a sexist creation by a male author."

For maximum effect, lead with a short, succinct statement.

Short starts are almost always best. Encompassing the idea to be discussed allows the audience to grasp the topic immediately and to stay interested. Most newspaper articles limit the opening paragraph to no more than thirty words; other types of writing should also aim to excite interest with the title or the first sentence. Readers of Terry McMillan's 1992 novel, *Waiting to Exhale*, for example, want to know who is holding her breath and why. Trigger interest in the title or first sentence, and more than half the job is done.

An especially weak start is a definition of the topic that begins with "According to Webster's." As a generic name for dictionaries, *Webster's* can mean any dictionary on the market, and the quality of definitions ranges widely from one dictionary to the next. At the least, the specific Webster's should be identified to give the start more power, perhaps through noting the difference in definitions between, say, a Merriam-Webster's dictionary and Webster's II.

Following are two dozen of the weakest words for starting. Overcome these false leads, and the ability to begin with power will improve any writing or speaking.

POWER STOPS

"First off" — This prepositional phrase loses power for every user; replace it with *First,* or lose it altogether.

"I don't mean to pry, but" — Watch out for this disclaimer; it always introduces a prying question.

"I'm not complaining, but" — The user, of course, is getting ready to complain.

"As a matter of fact" — Eliminate these unnecessary words; facts need no introduction.

"Before I start" — Here is a sneaky way for speakers to prolong the agony.

"If you ask me" — This introduction shows that nobody asked.

"If you don't mind my saying so" — What is said is almost always minded.

"No disrespect intended" — This start paves the way to disrespect.

"Speaking objectively" — Translate this phrase as "in my biased opinion."

"To begin with" — The phrase wastes words; just begin.

"I want to thank you" — Simply use *thank you;* the verb *want* implies an inability to thank.

"I'd really like to add" — The implied words to follow are "but I can't"; either add whatever is going to be said or drop it.

"What if I were to tell you . . . ?" — This question may or may not be true; the wording places truth in doubt.

"How would you feel if . . . ?" — Here is another opener for a question that may not be true.

"I hate to bring this up, but" — Usually the writer or speaker of this expression is eager to bring it up.

"Let me be honest" — This lead suggests that the user has been dishonest up to this point.

"Don't get angry, but" — Most of the words that follow this opening tend to anger the listener.

"You know what your problem is?" — The audience is on the defensive before the problem is named.

"This may be a stupid question" — This manipulative opener puts the audience in the position of reassuring the user instead of answering the question.

"I'm probably way off here" — Another self-deprecating introduction, this one may make the audience question the user's competence.

"You call that a . . . ?" — This type of question usually puts the listener on the defensive.

"You're not going to believe this" — The audience is already wondering whether to believe before the startling information is revealed.

"Now don't think I'm crazy, but" — Again, this type of introduction makes the audience question the user.

"I'm not one to brag, but" — This starting point almost always leads to bragging.

16

FOCUS

STAYING IN SHAPE

THE PRISONER STANDS before the firing squad of the French Foreign Legion. Before the execution can begin, the leader steps forward to ask the prisoner whether he wants a blindfold. The prisoner declines. "Cigarette?" Again, the prisoner says no. The leader asks one last question: "What do you want on your Tombstone?"

This scene, familiar to viewers of a television ad for frozen pizza, illustrates the difficult challenge in focusing. Just as the headline writer must reduce the lengthy article into a few catchy words, the tombstone inscriber must capture the life of the individual, or at least that person's most significant achievements, in a short epitaph. Thomas Jefferson, who wrote his own epitaph, marked the three achievements he considered his most important accomplishments, and being president was not among them. Dorothy Parker was much more succinct: "Excuse my dust."

Writers and speakers need that same focus, if not on the cosmic values of their existence, at least in recognizing the salient points of their messages. Being able to compress any message into a short headline or title helps indicate the direction that writing or speaking should take. Conversely, the inability to determine the importance of the message can often signal a lack of certainty or conviction by the word user.

"KEEP IT SHORT AND SIMPLE"

This World War II saying, frequently shortened to the acronym KISS, has many variations, but the sense is always the same. The longer the message, the poorer it will be received. Boiling down prose is almost always productive, and the inability to shorten the wording any further marks the refinement of the words to their shortest possible form.

Like the choice of short and simple words, the ability to focus the material in a short and simple style allows the most power with the fewest words. There are many techniques for emphasizing the message. In print, the main words may be underlined or italicized; in speech, the words may be spoken louder or after a significant pause. Finding the best ways to emphasize the message will pay off for the word user.

A young couple was overhead discussing a sermon on their way out of church. The husband called it "a great talk," and the wife agreed. When somebody who had not attended asked about the sermon, though, neither husband nor wife could remember the subject for that day. No "great talk" is easily forgotten; the message should be underscored for the audience or the meaning may be lost. When the message is memorably short, communication lacks complication.

Remember to "keep it short and simple." Breaking this rule for any reason can be the kiss of death.

STAY ON TRACK

Invited to give an after-dinner speech, a business executive in the food industry prepared for his talk by learning as much about the group and the dinner as he could. He wanted to move the audience gently from the meal to his speech on food and health. Finding that the dinner would be an all-you-can-eat buffet, he served a perfect opening line. "My doctor told me to watch my waist," he announced, patting his waistline, "and, thanks to what I've just eaten, it's finally out where I can see it." The secret of planning is to focus the listener or reader on the message. Words should be chosen that create interest and stay relevant to the topic. That same opening line might draw a laugh at a gathering of accountants or construction workers, but it works best as an anecdote leading into a discussion of healthful eating.

Focus the wording by deciding what the main message is and choosing terms that will emphasize it. Anything irrelevant should be eliminated.

A student asks how to write an essay about Julius Caesar. There are many possible approaches to Caesar for discussion: the historical Caesar, the importance of the Caesars in Roman civilization, the figure of Julius Caesar as envisioned in Shakespeare's play, and so on. Finding the limits of the discussion, often through determining the title for the essay, allows the writer or speaker to dismiss or downplay the plethora of details not connected to the topic at hand.

Prime topics for power language will track development or growth. In business reports, the decline or growth of a business should be emphasized and explained. Anything that stays the same will probably be boring; change, however, sparks drama and conflict. Look for a common thread that can show growth and change. An article about Eugene O'Neill, for example, may focus on the changing imagery of the moon from his early play *The Moon of the Caribbees* to his late drama *A Moon for the Misbegotten*.

That sense of movement pervades power language. The added force is best shown by comparing two approaches to the same topic, such as a hymn written two centuries ago. A dull essay may note that John Newton wrote the hymn "Amazing Grace." A lively essay, tracking change and growth, will explain that

Newton wrote the popular hymn after repenting his career as captain of a slave ship and converting to a strict religious life.

Once the limit is properly set, any example of writing or speaking will stay within it, and the title will not mislead the audience. Here is the significance of a first draft, which frequently helps the writer understand the main points worth discussing. From that initial draft come the limits for the second draft, leading away from digression and toward consistency.

As an aid to understanding, tracking marks the logical flow of an argument or explanation. A magazine writer discussing an emotional issue covers one side of the controversy, then explains the other side, and ends, "That settles it." Nothing, however, was settled. If that type of conclusion must be reached, the writer needs to go back and decide which side is preferable and support that decision with facts and further detail. Without that support, the train of thought fails to stay on track.

FOLLOW THROUGH THOROUGHLY

The best plan for writing or speaking is often found in titles or headlines, which condense a long story into a few words. After completing the first draft, the writer will find that a simple check of the written words against the proposed title will tell whether the title has helped focus the material. Any and all incidental material should either be cut from that first draft or be relegated to positions of lesser importance in the finished product.

Often a draft will be longer than the writing or speech should be. The material trimmed may be used for a separate piece or may need to be discarded. A love for the writer's or speaker's own words should not be a consideration in deciding which material is worthy of keeping.

If the second draft adheres more closely to the title, the result of that focus will be a much more powerful product. Another approach is to rework the title to reflect the limits of the finished essay, but any piece of writing or speaking that contains constant digression may not easily be pinned down to a title of a few words. Any title that requires more than a dozen words suggests a lack of focus; whittle it down, keeping the gist without making a list.

To help the audience focus, use a simple trick of direct address. "You Must Remember This" is almost an alternate title for the song "As Time Goes By," and the listener is immediately drawn into the lyrics. Interjections such as *yes* and *no* may also point the way: "Yes, Virginia," the editorial writer begins his most important clause, "there is a Santa Claus." Note that words such as *look* and *listen* also introduce the important material for the audience.

"KNOW WHEN TO SAY WHEN"

Listen to another commercial: "Know when to say when." This message began as a warning about drinking and driving. Moderation, however, is important as well to writers and speakers, and the best ones know when they have said enough. A student scribbles a note at the end of a rambling essay: "Please forgive how long this goes on. My mind is faster than my pen."

Grant proposals and student essays are often assigned a length. Other forms have no limits built in and must be concluded whenever the message has been communicated. Knowing when that point has been reached may be as easy as checking the final sentences against the title. In a successful communication, the message will be repeated and perhaps emphasized in the closing words. If the words at the end have nothing to do with the title and the first sentences, power is lost, and the word user should reconsider the supposedly complete effort.

Whenever words are out of focus, language produces humorous exchanges. Take the two comics who are playing carpenters.

One holds a nail and hands the other a hammer, all the while explaining to his reluctant partner, "When I nod my head, you hit it." The head is invariably hit, followed by a heated discussion of unclear pronoun reference.

Focus the language by choosing the right words. The following sentences show words out of focus. After each example of blurred words, though, comes the sharper choice.

THE BLURRED WORD

"We will be open until Saturday, weather permitted." (Weather will happen, *permitted* or not; the proper wording for this situation is *weather permitting*.)

"After the enemy attack, the army was surprised to find its forces decimated." (Originally, *decimate* meant "to reduce by a tenth"; most conquering armies prefer the sense of "to destroy overwhelmingly," and any user of *decimate* should be clear about the word's meaning in context.)

"The French language is lovely and gentile." (Regardless of the religion of the person who is speaking French, this language should be referred to as "lovely and *genteel*.")

"*Lowfat* means at least three grams of fat per serving." (To make this definition logical, the user must make the content "at *most* three grams of fat"; *at least* implies that more would be acceptable.)

"His zany stunts — i.e., the time he played basketball on a bicycle — have made him famous." (Abbreviations are also subject to blurring; the Latin *i.e.* stands for "that is" and should be followed by an explanation. Here the proper abbreviation is *e.g.*, to lead into an example.)

"The international arms trade is always full of pratfalls." (There are not many comic falls in arms trading; the proper word is *pitfalls*.)

"I think about the enormity of the mansion." (Purists hold *enormity* to mean "extreme sinfulness," not "extreme size"; unless the house is bought with stolen money, the user probably means "the *enormousness* of the mansion.")

"Two fractions of teens were fighting." (There are no halves of teens; the word here should be *factions*.)

"Your project sounds very ambitious, and I want to be apart." (Sometimes clarity comes with separating a solid word into two parts; apart means "away from," and the clearer wording would be a part for somebody who wants to be involved.)

"Baking the best everyday." (This fragment for a baker's advertisement is also blurred by pushing two words together. *Everyday* means "common, nothing special"; the baker would prefer to be known for baking fresh products *every day*.)

"The new estimate was seven times smaller than the old one." (Mathematicians will explain that "one time smaller" reduces something to nothing, and "seven times smaller" is meaningless; reduce this complicated wording to "one-seventh the size of the old one.")

"Her new portrait was hanged in the long hallway." (Criminals have been executed by being *hanged*; reserve that past tense for people and use *hung* for portraits and other objects.)

"You have no inclination of what that man has done." (The noun *inclination* means "leaning"; here the clearer word appears to be either *indication* or *inkling*.)

"The parties in the lawsuit expected the judge to be uninterested." (Unless the parties wanted a bored judge, the proper word for "unbiased" is *disinterested*.)

"It's an album that is a wonderful retribution to the composer." (The noun *retribution* often suggests "revenge"; here the simpler word needed is *tribute*.)

"The principal pointed out that the students continued to flaunt the rules." (The verb *flaunt* shows off ostentatiously; the verb *flout*, clearly the better choice, disregards deliberately.)

17

QUESTIONS

GRIPPING QUERIES

"WE LIVE IN a time," Hillary Clinton said at a news conference, "when there is a great deal of question raising." Not every question, however, is worth asking. When a guest tries to register at a hotel, he becomes impatient when told there is no record of his reservation. "I called ahead," he protests, and his anger rises when the clerk asks, "On the phone?"

Knowing which question to ask and how to ask it transforms aimless wording into pointed information seeking. Journalists are trained in "the Five W's and the H," shorthand for five questions that begin with the letter *W* (Who? What? When? Where? Why?) and the separate *H* question (How?). A solid lead for a news article, journalists learn, should answer those questions, because that information is what the reader looks for first.

The article itself is often written in what has come to be called inverted pyramid style. That upside-down pyramid is wide at the top, narrowing down to the least important information by the conclusion of the article. Editors can therefore lop off the end of a piece that runs too long, and the reader will not be cheated of the most significant facts.

Although power language does not require the inverted pyramid style, those six leading questions still solicit the most important information in the least time. Notice that none of those questions will solicit a *yes* or *no* response; each requires information or at least opinion. Learning how to ask the right questions will propel both writing and speaking toward more power.

ASK WHAT NEEDS TO BE ASKED

Nothing else causes words to veer off course faster than unnecessary information. When focus fails, side issues mislead the audience and create a lack of trust in the source. Some questions are not meant to solicit information. Ask the harmless "How are you?" and risk getting an entire medical report. Similarly, restaurateurs may hear more than they want with the simple query "And how was your meal?" Instead, the writer or speaker needs to point questions in the right direction.

Do rhetorical questions work? These questions, asked by somebody who also plans to answer them, may help direct the reader's attention. The question that begins this paragraph, for instance, allows the subject to be raised and insists that the rest of the paragraph be devoted to its answer. How often should rhetorical questions be used? The answer is rarely, and almost never two in the same paragraph; two in the same essay or speech, in fact, would be pushing it.

Make sure that the form of the question allows for the proper answer. Questions that may be answered *yes* or *no* are often least effective in interviews, because the person responding may choose to take the shortest way out. "Do you believe your policy is best?" put to a politician may produce no more than a single-syllable affirmative response. "Why do you believe your policy is best?" may produce a book-length answer. The middle ground may well be "What short answer would you give a voter who wants to know why your policy is best?"

The wise candidate will give a short answer, suitable for sound bites on the evening news. An unreasonably long answer, of course, reveals more about the politician than any number of other questions might. The inability to respond well to what is asked has caused candidates to lose elections.

DIRECT THE ANSWERS

The humor columnist Erma Bombeck knows how to get the right reaction from a question. A 1978 collection of her essays sports the pointed title *If Life Is a Bowl of Cherries, What Am I Doing in the Pits?*

Writers and speakers should learn how to ask questions, shouldn't they? The answer — "Yes, they should" — flows naturally from that query. That directing of a question at the end of a declarative statement is known as a tag question, and it can be an effective tool to get a desired answer. (Much weaker in style is the echo question, which simply parrots; a questioner asks, "How much did you pay for that?" and the response is the echoed "How much did I pay for it?")

Use tag questions as rarely as rhetorical questions, which allow a writer or speaker to ask an obvious question to set up an obvious answer. ("How do I love thee?" asks a poem by Elizabeth Barrett Browning. "Let me count the ways.") Too much direction in these questions may cause trouble. Lawyers object to "leading questions," asked in a certain way to prompt the desired answer. A district attorney may simplify any question to *yes* or *no* status by starting, "Did you or did you not." The danger comes in asking questions that trap the answerer, who may be ordered to respond *yes* or *no* to "Are you still a compulsive liar?"

"Do you mind?" is a simple question, with an equal chance of eliciting *yes* or *no*, depending on the responder's opinion. Much more powerful is the tag question of "You don't mind, do you?" to point the answer in the direction the questioner wishes to go.

It takes more confidence on the listener's part to refuse a tag question than to express an opinion on the shorter question. Use tag questions carefully, however. Once the listener balks and refuses to be guided by the tag question, that person is much more skeptical about the remainder of the message being conveyed. Putting a reader or listener on the defensive makes the word user's task all the more difficult.

A number of tag questions should be eliminated from a power vocabulary. The weakest candidates include the following:

1. O.K.?
2. You know?
3. See?
4. Right?
5. Get it?

The writer or speaker should be especially wary about tag questions in rhetorical questions, because such obvious leading may upset the audience.

ANSWER WHAT NEEDS TO BE ANSWERED

Everybody has seen politicians in action. Asked on the evening news about a controversial issue, a candidate sidesteps, responding with a packaged answer that fails to address the question. "Pollution problems are important," the politician begins, "and that reminds me of an equally serious issue. . . ."

The reverse side of asking a correct question is the need to answer the question correctly. The attention span of the average person may wander if a short discourse develops between the asking of the question and the specific answering of it. Leaving the listener in suspense may occasionally have its advantages, but for the direct communicating of a message, any question should be given the answer it deserves within a reasonable time.

Speakers who have packaged answers may well try to deliver their planned talk despite the topic of the question. Such answers tend to wander far afield and make the listener wonder whether the speaker knows the answer. "I suppose you could say so," a witness admits under cross-examination, trying hard to avoid *yes*, but most answers should not be convoluted. A simple, direct answer in debate or in telephone conversation reassures the listener of the answerer's ability to handle questions.

Occasionally an unasked question will be so obvious that the answer should be made available. A statement such as "Texas is the second largest state" may well leave the listener pondering what the largest state is, and the lost attention cuts into whatever the message about Texas is trying to convey. Slip in the answer to an unasked question, if leaving it unanswered will be distracting — "Texas is the second largest state (only Alaska is bigger)" — and the audience will be satisfied with the information provided.

Once the question has been answered, however, move on to the next issue. A nineteenth-century novelist stops in the middle of a long and obvious digression in the story to say, "Why tell the rest?" The reader already knows where the story is leading, and enough information has been supplied. Remember: "Know when to say when."

Phrasing the answer requires paying particular attention to the wording of the question. In Washington, a congressman is asked whether ignorance or apathy is the bigger problem. "I don't know," he says, "and I don't care."

In lawyer-bashing, stories are told of the client who asks his high-profile attorney about his rate and is told that three questions cost $10,000. When the client balks, asking if that isn't a bit expensive, the lawyer replies, "Yes. What's your final question?"

Watch the wording of questions. The everyday use of contractions gives way in more polished writing or speaking. The normal "wouldn't it?" is often turned into the formal "would it not?"

Not all questions are equal. Perhaps the most wasteful form of questioning is the unnecessary raising of the voice at the end of a declarative sentence. Taking "I'll see you at three" and turning it into "I'll see you at three?" gives all the power to the other person, almost always a mistake.

Among the most frequent mistakes questioned by teachers are sentences that violate the standards of good English usage. Some broken rules seem harmless; others may be dangerous. A product that advertises "This protective gear is guaranteed inflammable" may expect lawsuits, because *inflammable* means the same as *flammable*.

What follows are twenty examples of the substandard usages that teachers question and editors detest. The more acceptable the wrong words may seem, the more work should be done to overcome these bad habits. Use these errors only in trying to provoke a question or perhaps a violent reaction to language. In the presence of an English teacher, never substitute "graduated high school" for "graduated *from* high school" or pronounce "library" as if it were "liberry," mistakes that sound worse than nails on a blackboard.

THE LOWEST SCORE

"The coach plans to make the team practice Saturday, irregardless of their performance today." (The substandard *irregardless* contains the double negative of the prefix *ir-* and the suffix *-less;* reduce the negatives to "regardless" for an acceptable alternative.)

"Me and her used to have fun at the beach." (Heard all too often these days, this error in grammar tries to turn objects into subjects; the proper pronouns would start this sentence as "She and I used to.")

"Nobody can say for certain when he snuck into the room."
(The proper past tense for the verb *sneak* is *sneaked.*)

"By the time the ship reached the next port, the newest passenger was nauseous." (Unless the newest passenger made people seasick, the proper adjective is *nauseated;* think of *nauseous* as a synonym for *nauseating.*)

"Hopefully, the ski slopes will have enough snow by tomorrow." (Purists hate *hopefully* as a sentence adverb meaning "it is to be hoped"; instead, somebody or something should be "full of hope," as in "Hopefully, the skiers awaited reports of a major snowstorm to come.")

"Reaction Mixed on Affect on U.S. Relations." (This newspaper headline loses effect by trying to turn the verb *affect* into a noun for "result"; the correct noun is *effect.*)

"There were some awful good reasons for what we did." (If the overused *awful* must be included in this sentence, then it should at least be as the adverb *awfully* to modify the adjective *good.*)

"The experiment was expected to study the effects of 'nuke-yoo-ler' energy." (Few words grate on the ears of audiences as much as this mispronunciation of *nuclear;* pronounce it "*noo*-klee-er" to avoid any explosions.)

"Across the generations, this secret has held it's power and kept family members in line." (The contraction *it's* means "it is" or "it has"; for the proper possessive form of *it,* use *its* — no apostrophe.)

"The media has been tracking this news story for almost three months now." (A word of Latin pedigree, *media* is a plural form of *medium;* never use "media has" or "media is" in place of the proper plurals, "media have" and "media are.")

"He played really good in the opening match." (The adverb *really* adds little meaning to the sentence; even worse, though, an action verb such as *played* must be modified by an adverb: "He played really well.")

"Between you and I, the administration should not have demanded a dress code for the students." (Hypersensitive users of the subject pronoun *I* should not try to force it into becoming an object; "between you and *me*" is the only proper form for this prepositional phrase.)

"Cuts in the budget may mean less officers patrolling the streets in the near future." (Whatever else is cut, a countable noun such as *officers* takes the modifier *fewer*, not *less*; supermarket signs for "Ten items or less" are also wrong.)

"The six difficult chores left the worker with a dilemma." (No, a *dilemma* is a choice between two; with six choices, the worker faces a *problem* or at least a *challenge*.)

"The phone rang earlier, but I don't know whom answered it." (The *who-whom* dilemma proves difficult for many. Remember that the pronoun must work in its own clause, and "whom answered it" is as wrong as "him answered it" would be; use *who* instead.)

"He said he plans to give the book to myself." (The reflexive *myself* has no *me* in the sentence to emphasize; use the simpler *me*, and save *myself* for the rare occasions that require emphasis.)

"The nurse checked the patients and said they appeared to be alright." (There is no single word *alright*; the proper words are *all right*, and any other spelling is all wrong.)

"Several tutors were trying to help learn him the material." (Teachers and tutors do not *learn* a student the material; they may, however, try to *teach him* or *help him learn*.)

"She tries to serve them healthy food as much as possible." (Purists avoid *healthy* to describe products that make people healthy; instead, those products are *healthful*.)

"That ain't the first time he made the mistake." (Use *ain't* only to get a predictable reaction out of the language police, who prefer *is not*.)

18

ANSWERS

FACT AND FRICTION

NOËL COWARD WAS not impressed. Reading prose by James Bond's creator disturbed the British wit, who wrote directly to Ian Fleming. "I am even willing to forgive your reckless use of invented verbs," Coward told him, ". . . but what I will neither accept nor forgive is the highly inaccurate statement that when it is eleven A.M. in Jamaica, it is six A.M. in dear old England. When it is eleven A.M. in Jamaica, it is four P.M. in dear old England, and it is carelessness of this kind that makes my eyes slits of blue."

Readers will forgive much, every writer learns, but one thing they will not forgive is a factual error. Accuracy counts. No matter how powerful the language and technically convincing the argument may be, writing or speaking will come to a halt in the face of a mistake. Even the great American novel may be derided if it names Baltimore as the capital of Maryland (the capital is Annapolis).

Writers and speakers must check the facts of their material, because nothing else destroys an audience's confidence so fast as an obvious error. To hold on to the power generated in writing or speaking, the word user must be as sure of accuracy as possible, given the constraints of deadlines and human error. Those who rely on wording to hide error will be disappointed.

As a matter of fact, facts matter. Three prominent keys mark the power language of facts, and friction occurs whenever they are ignored.

OFFER OPINIONS JUDICIOUSLY

A judge offers an opinion only after all the facts have been presented and weighed, and a good writer or speaker will follow that lead. Even in an editorial that is primarily an opinion piece, the blatant presentation of opinion should have at least as much fact as feeling. Readers and listeners have opinions of their own, and those are often in stark contrast to the ideas being presented.

The writer or speaker should look first for common ground, and knowing the audience helps produce some common ideas or interests. From that point, the introduction of opinion should be done in ways that will not cause the audience to close its collective mind on the topic. Blanket statements and biased generalizations ("All books are evil") cannot help sparking doubt.

Opinions, like statistics, are best used in small numbers, saved for their most effective moments. Blind attacks are similarly unfair; a political advertisement describes an opponent's record in dispassionate terms and then adds, "Too many politicians are corrupt," making a strong, unsupported implication that that opponent is corrupt. Instead, use specific details throughout to support an argument, and save the personal opinions for editorializing.

Some speakers try to offer damage control for their own opinions. They begin odd facts with "strangely enough" or "in a funny sort of way," or couch opinions with "I think" or "it seems to me" or even "in my humble opinion." These phrases may block criticism, but they also tend to remove the force from whatever follows.

When opinions are to be used, brutal frankness has a power to it. Consider a florist's billboard in Florida: "Shakespeare would have written her a poem. You're not Shakespeare." Judge carefully whether opinion helps or hurts the message.

CITE STATISTICS CONSERVATIVELY

In the late nineteenth century, Mark Twain attributed to Benjamin Disraeli, the British prime minister, a list of the three main categories of dishonesty: "lies, damned lies, and statistics." Almost any statistic can be produced, whether true or not, to back up an argument, and the more statistics given, the faster an audience's attention will wander. In the midst of a debate on the Vietnam War, a speaker had time called on him when he spent his entire ten minutes reeling off the costs of equipment and weaponry. Not only had the audience members stopped listening, but also that type of verbal abuse may well have swayed their support to the other side.

Statistics do have their usefulness, though. A specific figure or two may be offered, especially if the source is reliable and identified, to support the ideas expressed. In fact, such a number may impress the audience that the speaker or writer has done the homework to back up the phrases with facts.

The trouble comes with overuse. Remember the word *conservatively.* This adverb limits the speaker or writer to err in the direction of underplaying the numbers. Figure that more than three statistics in any short essay or speech may well undermine the intended effect on the audience.

Also, confine the information to a specific topic. John Bunyan had more leeway in *Pilgrim's Progress:* "I will talk of things heavenly, or things earthly; things moral, or things evangelical; things sacred, or things profane; things past, or things to come; things foreign, or things at home; things more essential, or things circumstantial." A business memorandum, however, has its priorities, and the word user should respect them. Consider the down-to-earth detail in ads for Pony Express riders in 1860: "Wanted — young, skinny, wiry fellows, not over eighteen. Must be expert riders, willing to risk death daily. Orphans preferred."

When offering statistics, be sure to give context with text. Photojournalists know how to take pictures of the same campaign rally from different angles to suggest that either a large crowd is listening or only a small contingent supports the candidate. Neither view is fair, and wording has the same requirement for fairness; give the full context to make the facts work properly.

Equally powerless are attempts to hide the opposing view or to fail to address the opposite side of an issue. Even if most of the experts fall on the word user's side, their expertise often comes across as merely more opinions, and certainly a writer or speaker should attempt to show how the other side fails to make its case. Sometimes the most effective use of expertise comes from quoting an authority who disagrees about the topic. The writer or speaker may then attack that opposing position, telling why it should be disregarded and the opposite view upheld.

Many people dislike being told how to think, even if experts hold the view. Remember to limit such "evidence" in any attempt to persuade the reader or listener. When presenting information as fact, be sure that it can be supported. "Few politicians believe" is a poor qualifier, because there is no way of knowing what few politicians believe. Similarly, "some say" or "some criticize" offers no sense of who is doing the talking, and the information conveyed is often only an opinion, perhaps the writer's or speaker's.

Provide proof, and make it specific enough to count. "I'm flying to Burlington" may sound specific, but unless the listener knows that the destination is Burlington, Iowa, or Burlington, Vermont, communication falters.

Of course, proof is needed whenever a case is being presented. No lawyer who is competent would want to press a court case without obtaining as much proof as possible. Find the most important evidence for the position being argued. Then organize it in the most efficient way possible, saving the strongest evidence for the final point. That organization leads the reader or listener to the conclusion, proving the point without battering.

The problem occurs with opposing proof. Sometimes this evidence is ignored or slighted in the text. The strongest cases, however, will try to explain that discrepancy, counting on the audience's intelligence to weigh the proof against the interpretation.

Also, watch the tone in offering information and suggestions. A phone message stated, "You will receive a memo today, and you will respond to it tomorrow." That imperious tone will negate the listener's interest — unless, of course, the boss is calling.

That tone of officiousness also creeps in with the use of qualifiers such as *of course* and *as you know* and even *obviously.* A comedy show ended properly with the statement "Our guest star, of course, was Bob Hope." Less defensible is a statement such as "Shakespeare's last play was, of course, *The Tempest.*" That statement may or may not be true; even if it is true, it is not so widely acknowledged that the information should *of course* be known. Saying it is "Shakespeare's best play, of course," offers only opinion and is equally questionable. Similarly, "The word *antepenultimate* means, obviously, 'third from the end'" can make the audience feel ignorant. Condescending to an audience, and doing it obviously, may lose the audience entirely.

CORRECT MISTAKES LIBERALLY

Whenever a mistake is made, the most powerful antidote is self-correction. Often discouraged as a form of losing power, the catching of errors should be praised as a sign of the control and carefulness of the word user. It is far better to correct the word user's own error than to allow somebody else the satisfaction of contradicting.

The conservative radio host Rush Limbaugh said of a politician, "They don't call him Slick for anything," then stopped and corrected his mistake, "— for nothing." A guest on another talk show stopped herself in midsentence as she said, "It's something that very little people — very *few* people know." Perhaps the only way to avoid such mistakes in speaking is to take extra time between sentences. As Thomas Jefferson explained, "Delay is preferable to error."

Everybody makes mistakes. Perhaps the most serious ones, though, occur after the initial error, when the person digs in and stubbornly refuses to admit the mistake. Instead, mistakes should be acknowledged openly and generously.

Credit should be given not only to the person who has caught the mistake but also to the strength of the correction itself. A college professor had been misspelling the Greek concept of *hamartia* as *harmatia* until a bold graduate student pointed out the mistake. From that point on, the teacher made an extra effort in using the word to indicate the proper spelling. Learning from mistakes and making a real effort to keep the correction front and center show the power of education at its best.

Before offering any information as fact, be sure that it is correct. "There's never been a woman Grand Master chess player," asserted a conservative politician; correctors came from everywhere to point out at least two women who made the "fact" false.

Also, be sure that the statement is logical. Making a sentence too elliptical by leaving out essential words can destroy the logic. "Twenty-one percent of girls," an Ohio newspaper reported on school dropouts, "said they left because they had become a mother, as did eight percent of boys."

The logical communication of facts takes effort. Every writer or speaker should try to avoid the criticism Lord Byron leveled against another writer's attempt to explain a poem. "I wish," Byron wrote, "he would explain his explanation."

Lead the listener or reader into the important information. To focus an answer, try a brief phrase followed by a colon and an explanation. "Winter is more severe this season," a weather report begins. "The reason: Winds out of the west have been unusually strong. . . ."

Exactness counts with facts, and writers cannot get much more exact than Herman Melville's narrator in *Moby Dick*, who pinpoints the exact time of his storytelling: "Down to this blessed minute (fifteen and a quarter minutes past one o'clock P.M. of this sixteenth day of December, A.D. 1851)."

Facts must be expressed in the right words, but all too often the wrong word comes to mind first. Errors lurk in the sentences below. Each example is followed by the correction, with fact-fixing as a major ingredient of power language.

In the list that follows, watch for the wrong word and consider the correction that follows. Too often the word that is wrong leads to a meaning that is wronged. Remember, though, that the right word may depend on the location. "Take a decision," perfectly normal in British English, is properly corrected in American English to "make a decision."

THE WRONG WORD

"I suppose this qualifies as a emergency." (The article *a* should not be used before a word beginning with a vowel sound; make it "*an* emergency.")

"We watched an 1940 film." (Even though the year is expressed

in numerals, it is pronounced with an initial *n* sound —
"nineteen-forty" — and should be preceded by *a* before that
consonant sound: "*a* 1940 film.")

"The minister delivered an eulogy that surprised the congregation." (Although *eulogy* begins with a vowel, the opening
sound — *yoo* — begins with a consonant, and *a* is correct:
"*a* eulogy.")

"Remember that it takes two to tangle." (Any number of people
may tangle; remember the expression is "it takes two to
tango.")

"I know that I'm at fault, and I'm not trying to make amends."
(This apparent apology seems to need *excuses* in place of
amends, or else the apologizer is not sincerely sorry.)

"Send that package first-class to extradite it." (The police may
extradite a criminal from one area to another; to speed up
the mail, the verb *expedite* is needed.)

"Each speaker stood at the podium to deliver a speech." (A
podium is the raised platform speakers stand on; instead,
each speaker may have stood "at the *lectern*" or "*on* the
podium" to deliver a speech.)

"The voters of this district feel that the new tax is inequitous
and atrocious." (If the tax is sinful, it is *iniquitous*; if unfair,
it is *inequitable*, not *inequitous*.)

"That word illicits images of children at play." (Something *il-
licit* is unlawful or wrong; the verb for producing or drawing
out images is *elicits*.)

"The store is noisome and makes it difficult to hear even a loud
conversation." (The adjective *noisome* — meaning "offensive, disagreeable" — may apply here, but the level of
sound should properly be described as *noisy*.)

"This bureaucracy has taken the very same tact." (*Tact* is diplomacy at its best; instead, the bureaucracy has repeated an
old mistake by taking the very same *tack*.)

"We need to give children parameters so they'll know what's
expected of them." (The term *parameters* comes from

mathematics and should never be confused with *perimeters*, a synonym for "boundaries.")

"A survey of the perspective jurors revealed some unusual attitudes about the case." (A point of view is a *perspective*; here the proper adjective is *prospective*, for jury candidates who may be selected for duty.)

"That report is incredulous, and you cannot expect people to believe it." (The report may be *incredible*, and people may be *incredulous* about what it says, but the report itself cannot be *incredulous*.)

"He came to the schools in both towns yesterday afternoon." (The verb *came* can be used only for approaching the user; the proper verb here is *went*.)

"The workers emigrated to America and soon found opportunities for work." (Use *emigrated* if the emphasis is on leaving a country, as in "emigrated from Ireland"; this sentence emphasizes the arrival in America and should use *immigrated*.)

"She left early to bring the report to her office." (The verb *bring* also requires approaching the user; this movement is not toward the user and should take the verb *take*.)

"The attorney introduced the evidence to refute the opponent's case and hopes to win the lawsuit." (Until the argument is settled in that attorney's favor, the evidence can hope only to *rebut* or "argue against"; save *refute* for a definite decision favoring that attorney.)

"Japan imports more than just great cars." (This billboard for Japanese beer in America says the opposite of what it means, because *imports* brings into the country; to the United States, Japan "*exports* more than just great cars.")

"She likes to hone in on the intricate details." (The verb *hone* sharpens; the expression for coming closer is "*home* in on.")

"Searchers took to the water in hopes of finding the floundering ship." (No ship is likely to *flounder*, which means "to struggle or move clumsily"; instead, the ship was probably *foundering,* another word for "sinking.")

"They tried not to aggravate the mugger." (The verb *aggravate* means "to make worse or heighten," as in "aggravate the skin condition"; here the proper verb is *irritate.*)

"The captain wanted to appraise the flight crew of the situation." (*Appraise* means "to rate or evaluate"; what the captain wanted to do was to inform or *apprise* the flight crew.)

"The couple expected to precede with the sale of the house in a few weeks." (To *precede* is to come before; to *proceed* is to go ahead, as in "*proceed* with the sale of the house.")

"Don't plan to go any farther in explaining your actions!" (The proper word is *further;* save *farther* to describe physical distance, not a higher degree.)

"He felt terribly about causing the dent in the car." (A person with numb fingers may feel *terribly;* here *feel* is used as a linking verb and takes the predicate adjective *terrible.*)

"Every two weeks she looks forward to receiving the bimonthly magazine." (*Bimonthly* means "every other month," not "every two weeks"; use *semimonthly* or *twice a month* for a two-week period.)

"The bus drove over twelve doctors going to the conference." (The bus "drove *over*" nobody; use *more than,* not *over,* with numbers.)

19

TECHNOLOGY

FAX CHECKING

"SORRY, WE CAN'T take your message," the secretary at a computer firm told telephone callers. "Our answering machine is broken."

If progress produces too much stress and tech talk sounds like a foreign language, do not despair — there are still ways to get the message across. Whether sending a memo by fax (making sure the paper is properly facing up or down) or posting a letter the old-fashioned way (now sometimes called "snail mail"), a writer may find the same rules apply in adding power to prose.

People who would not dream of stretching their facts have no qualms whatsoever about stretching their fax. In fact, some business writers seem to think that a fax should cover as much material as possible, with subjects that range from last winter's weather to next summer's baseball.

Follow four keys in faxing or whatever business communication is being used, and the words are well on their way to winning.

TELEGRAPH THE MESSAGE

More than in any other form of communication, a business communication should be brief and to the point. Making a request or giving an order sounds simple enough, but far too many writers fear the use of short words, as if simple words were evidence of a simple mind. As a result, turning a straightforward statement into a maze of bureaucratic jargon has become a dubious art form.

Take the massive memo recently displayed in a Maryland courthouse: "Contract maintenance personnel will implement State of Maryland code required cleaning of the judicial center's escalator system." The reader could have walked the three flights of stairs before realizing that the escalator was being cleaned.

Make the point in easily understood words, and the message travels at least twice as fast. The Wright brothers sent a telegram from Kitty Hawk in 1903, using simple words to describe their historic accomplishment: "Success / four flights Thursday morning / all against twenty-one-mile wind / started from level with engine power alone / average speed through air thirty-one miles / longest fifty-nine seconds / inform press / home Christmas." Emulate that compressed information (although perhaps not the writing style).

Too much condensation, in fact, leads to broken English. Cary Grant once received a telegram from a press agent asking, "How old Cary Grant?" The film actor telegraphed back, "Old Cary Grant fine. How you?"

GATHER THE EVIDENCE

"The way you win the most battles," a corporate vice president once said, "is to have information. Contrary to what people think, it's not having influence." An Ohio publisher agrees: "Information is the name of the game."

Having the information and conveying it quickly and force-fully will make the difference. To have the information, though, the prepared writer or speaker must first collect it. Time spent in research pays off, if only in giving the audience confidence in the word user's knowledge about the subject. Herman Melville may get away with supporting a fact with "says the old writer — of whose work I possess the only copy extant," but do not expect chief executive officers or English teachers to fall for that one.

Instead, make an extra effort to gather sufficient information. A White House aide was recently asked to name the three main activities of every working day. The aide replied, "Checking facts, paying attention to details, and meeting deadlines," all practical concerns regardless of the technology used.

In a lecture on writing, the novelist Shirley Jackson told of one result of failing to gather enough information. She received a fan letter and, thinking she recognized the correspondent's name as that of another writer, wrote back. Only later did she realize that the man's name was familiar — from newspaper accounts about his California trial for allegedly murdering his wife with an ax — and with dread she checked a copy of her letter back to him: "Thank you very much for your kind letter about my story. I admire *your* work, too."

POINT TO THE POINT

The most important business abbreviation is neither *Inc.* nor *Corp.* For the writer or speaker, the single most significant shortening must be the introductory term *Re.*

Decide what the proper message is and stick to it. *Re* at the start of a business document means "Regarding" and should be immediately followed by the gist of the message, expressed concisely in three or four words.

With this introduction, however, comes responsibility. The writer or speaker must telegraph the message after *Re* and then fulfill that promise in the actual communication. Once the reader or listener is primed for the facts to come, no fax should lead in other directions.

Stay focused. Too often, the writer of a fax or electronic letter takes on too much cargo for the words to fly. Any fax that discusses the weather, specifics about recent illness, the company's latest Christmas party, and the economic state of the union covers entirely too much territory. To reinforce the message, occasionally use short imperative phrases followed by colons. *Be warned* and *Make no mistake* are favorites in book reviews. *Remember* may also provide a gentle reminder.

Be sure, however, that the information being supplied is the same information that was requested. Planning a honeymoon, a couple sent away for information about Florida and received a brochure about a hotel in Toronto. Even worse, convention-goers tell horror stories of sending away for information about weekend accommodations at hotels and motels; instead, the convention bureau sent letters from local real estate agents offering to show houses to these "potential buyers."

REMEMBER THE MESSAGE

Always be sure that the message makes sense. Imagine the surprise of the humorist Jean Kerr in 1957 when she ordered tickets for "the first available Wednesday evening" of a hit musical and the theater returned her check. Outraged, she included her response in *Please Don't Eat the Daisies* as a letter to the theater management: "Do you mean to suggest that down through the echoing corridors of time there will never be a Wednesday night on which two seats will be available? I don't wish to inject an empty note of pessimism but even you . . . must concede that there is a possibility — at least in theory — that sometime, say in 1962, you might be willing, even anxious, to sell two seats."

Little disturbs a reader or listener more than words that fail to say what they mean or that seem to suggest the impossible. A mismanaged message is especially disturbing in business. During an average day of countless forms and faxes, a senseless letter stands out as an annoyance. Here is where a second reading helps to increase the power language. Even a swift proofreading job to shorten clauses and correct phrases adds clarity and may spare the embarrassment of sending a meaningless message.

Finding ways to underscore the message for the audience can help to achieve the word user's goal. "Help Wanted" ads, for example, are efficient because they use the fewest words possible to convey that message. Similar verbal pointers, from *Re* to *Listen up,* may give the added emphasis necessary to power the language.

Following are statements from business faxes and legal memos. Note how each is followed by a reworking guaranteed to increase the power of the message.

Business communications should be one step above grocery lists in conveying straightforward information. Knowing when and how to keep wordy phrases out of faxes and memos will save the senders as well as the receivers valuable time. Following are a dozen sentences worthy of shortening. Some need only a single word omitted; others would benefit from reworking for more precise wording.

MEANING BUSINESS

"Your pictures are just too perfect." (Perhaps *too good* may be used as a description; *perfect,* however, is an absolute word, unable to be qualified by a modifier such as *too.*)

"The report explained that the woman was a little pregnant at the time of the accident." (That reporter should also explain how somebody can be a "little pregnant"; like *perfect,* the absolute *pregnant* takes no qualifying other than *not.*)

"I used it to sort of relate to the students." (The expression *sort of* may be used to introduce a noun — "He bought a different sort of car" — but not to introduce a verb, even a verb as weak as *relate*.)

"He corrects anyone who says *ain't*. Only a fool would do that." (Does "only a fool" refer to the user of *ain't* or to the corrector? Make certain the second reference clearly reflects the first: "He corrects anyone who says *ain't*, a mistake only a fool would correct" or "He corrects anyone who says *ain't*, a word only a fool would use.")

"The second annual report was clearly more complete than the original." (Like *perfect* and *pregnant*, the adjective *complete* is an absolute and cannot be modified by *more* or *less*; substitute either *comprehensive* or *detailed*.)

"Prior to starting the seminar, she specialized in one-on-one tutorials in business management." (The faulty phrase here is the stuffy *prior to*; get down to business faster by trying the simpler *before*.)

"You'll find that corporate policy makes the use of outside equipment very impossible." (Once again, the absolute *impossible* should not take a qualifier; use *very* only to qualify words that can be described in degrees.)

"We've made a kind of a deal that is similar to previous dealings with that company." (Like *sort of*, the expression *kind of* should introduce only a noun, as it does here with *deal*; the article *a*, however, should come before only the word *kind*, not before *deal*: "We've made a kind of deal.")

"That publicity campaign fails to generate the same excitement as customer word-of-mouth does for free." (The prepositional phrase *for free* is a faulty combination of *free* and *for nothing*; free the sentence of the added *for* before *free*.)

"The fact remains that you should be in line for the next promotion." (Rarely does a *fact* need to be pointed out; the sentence benefits immediately from losing "The fact remains that": "You should still be in line. . . .")

"Do not expect to continue on with that same line of questioning." (There is no need for *on* to follow *continue*, which already means "to go on"; save space wherever possible, even with as short a word as *on*.)

"Financial wizards may be able to conjure up a solution to the current fiscal crisis." (*Conjure* needs no *up*; tightening the language of business communications will help unnecessary words disappear.)

20

WRITING

WINNING STYLE

"THERE'S NOTHING to writing," the sports columnist Red Smith once commented. "All you do is sit down at a typewriter and open a vein."

Fortunately, that degree of punishment is not necessary for most written communication. Writing should not be intensely painful, nor should it be considered a struggle or a contest with other writers. The comedian Fred Allen is credited with saying, "He writes so well, he makes me feel like putting my quill back into my goose." Usually, however, writers have only themselves to compete with in the process of creating their style.

What is style? Not even the great poets and literary critics can agree on an answer. Perhaps the most succinct explanation comes from the columnist William Safire in the *New York Times:* "The way you write reflects the way you think, and the way you think is the mark of the kind of person you are."

Raising that mark, however, takes effort and concentration. Recent reports indicate that students in the United States are losing writing skills. Even the Scholastic Aptitude Tests, long a staple of multiple-choice questions, have turned to written essays as a necessary gauge of a student's ability. Now more than ever, an important part of education is learning how to write clearly and effectively.

Many of the old techniques hold true in teaching power language. Writing should develop a topic sentence into a paragraph; the theme sentences of the opening paragraph should be explored in the later paragraphs of an essay. Structuring points with an outline is still the most effective way to communicate written information, but style is not so easily communicated.

Remember that no one person has any single style. Style varies from one writing situation to another. Even a simple list requires thought and precision; in fact, no other writing, not even Ernest Hemingway's, is so lean and practical as a grocery list. From grocery lists to annual reports, every person needs to find a writing style to fit the communicating.

Several strategies, however, can help to improve the writing, leading to more forceful communication.

WRITE TO A READER

"Literature is conversation written down," said one literary critic, and almost every form of writing improves with the introduction of a reader.

Even an imaginary reader helps, but knowing who will be reading a document helps the writer direct the message. If no reader is known or recognized, imagine writing to a pen pal or new acquaintance, and take the necessary care to convey information that may at first seem obvious or unnecessary. This writing forms the first draft, often written quickly to get the information down on paper; with that draft, the writer can rework the wording as needed to reach the final draft.

Be careful, though, that the tone of formal writing does not slip into the casual cadences of a letter to a friend. What the writer needs to envision is the person who receives the communication, somebody wanting to gain the information without puzzling over passages or needing to reread to make sense of the wording. Many modern writers use *you* to avoid the formal *one;* once *one* has been used, the writer is forced to stick to that impersonal pronoun ("One must do one's duty, mustn't one?"), sounding more formal than normal.

The first draft will probably be more casual than formal. Then the later versions should be reworked with the suitable tone for the occasion. With this strategy, even formal reports and student essays can become easier to write.

"I don't like to do drafts," a student says. "If I stop writing and put it away, how will I remember what I wanted to say?" A common problem for writers is a sense that everything must be placed on paper at once or the flow will be lost. Here is the important point for outlines, which allow the writer to retain ideas and to check for missing steps in an argument or explanation that may not be written until days later. For those who fear losing their place, try Hemingway's system; whenever his work was interrupted, he would leave off writing in midsentence, allowing him to pick up exactly where his words ended earlier. With such an approach, a first draft may be no more than a flushed-out outline.

Second and subsequent drafts take a more formal form. The formal paragraph has an introductory or topic sentence, sentences of development, and a conclusion; the formal essay has the same essential parts. Avoid convoluted sentences and phrasing that sounds unlike anything ever said. A reader prefers conversation to lecturing.

Reading is primarily a visual experience, and the writer should keep that reality in mind, if only for the sake of the reader. Long sentences can easily fall apart or force the reader to do the writer's work of straightening out the message. Too many long sentences in a row, outside James Joyce's novels, may discourage the reader's interest.

Vary the lengths of sentences. After any two or three long sentences, use a short one to make a concise point. Readers who tend to skim aim for these short sentences, which provide a prime spot for the most important information of the paragraph.

Similarly, long paragraphs may draw the reader's attention away from the writing. In formal discourse, a paragraph should always contain at least three sentences: the topic sentence, the development of that sentence, and the conclusion. Less formal writing has moved away from such restrictions, but that model gives the uncertain writer a form to follow.

SPELL CORRECTLY

In a Washington bookstore, an entire shelf is devoted to books on what a label calls SPELING. Yes, spelling counts. Speakers have the advantage over writers in this case; unless the text of the speech is being released in printed form, the speaker may get away with spelling phonetically, never differentiating among *two/to/too* or *their/they're/there*.

Spelling errors are noticed far more frequently in writing than in speaking. Unless a word is mispronounced, for example, the audience may never know of a speaker's inability to spell the word. Typographical errors occur all too often when extra letters sneak in and out of words. A reference book indexes a quotation on "words writ in waters" as "words writ in waiters." Word comes from a school that the staff will be getting not a "copying machine" but a "coping machine"; the lost *y* confused some parents and perhaps raised the hopes of frazzled teachers.

Food terms seem to cause the most spelling trouble. Restaurant menus have turned chocolate mousse into "chocolate mouse" and Hunan cuisine into "Human cuisine." A college student, writing on the force of metaphor, created new food for thought with "meataphor." Sometimes the writer may add a space to a word that should be solid, leaving one food critic "out standing in his field." Even transposed letters may cause problems, such as when a new bran diet led to the nutrition report that the dieters "ate the barn for breakfast."

Of course, spelling should count for speakers too, but writers are at an obvious disadvantage. A new medication, for example, was given with this written explanation: "This will clam you down." That transposing of letters would do little to calm the reader. Not every typographical error will be caught, but the fewer left in the final product, the better the communicating.

PUNCTUATE PROPERLY AND CLEARLY

Writers must be equally diligent with proper punctuation. A middle school student, wanting to run for class president, was asked to list the reasons for his campaign. He omitted what his teacher probably considered an essential comma between two of his infinitive phrases: "to help the teacher to learn responsibility." (Notice how the meaning changes with the comma properly placed after "teacher," turning one reason into two.)

The bulletin from a large church comments on "each others' good times and bad, each others joys and sorrows, each other's heavy loads." Only the last phrase has the proper apostrophe.

Punctuation should be to the point, and the less needed, the better. If a word is broken at the end of the line, aim to separate the syllables with a hyphen; one newspaper tried "rea-dout," an unacceptable break for *readout*. When a comma or period is required, leaving it out will also hurt the message. Adding extra marks, from unnecessary exclamations (!!!) to endless ellipses (. . .), similarly counts against the communication.

Capitalization, like spelling, is a problem for writers, not speakers. Avoid the extensive capitalization used by Emily Dickinson or the lowercasing of e. e. cummings. Also, be consistent in using capital letters; inconsistency mars this notice for a business meeting: "Be Sure to attend This session."

To reach a strong conclusion, go back to the beginning and reread the introduction. The end of the writing should indicate that the writer is still aware of the way it began. A strong anecdote or compelling reason should be saved for the final paragraphs, leaving the reader to feel that whatever has been said was worth reading.

Once the writing is completed, the rewriting begins. Contemplate the century-old advice of the British author Sydney Smith: "As a general rule, run your pen through every other word you have written; you have no idea what vigor it will give your style."

A message can speak to the reader only as well as the writer has committed it to paper. While speech allows other clues to meaning, the written passage has no vocal tone or inflection to aid the reader. The proverb that compares a picture to a thousand words may be overestimating the value of those words unless the writer has taken time to make the words meaningful.

Below are passages from college and business writing that show punctured punctuation deflating the meaning of the sentences. Each is followed by the corrected punctuation, too late to save the message.

MECHANICAL FAILURES

"I think you'd better tell her Secretary." (This advice, meant for the secretary of state, desperately needs its comma: "I think you'd better tell her, Secretary.")

"For cleaning razors with our compliments." (This phrase on paper towels for a hotel chain would benefit from at least a dash after *razors* — unless the compliments are on the razors.)

"Her first marriage to the company president ended in divorce." (Unless she was married twice to the same man, commas are needed to make sense of this sentence: "Her first marriage, to the company president, ended in divorce.")

"Politics was not his first choice — he wanted a chance — actually several chances — to play football." (Dashes should be used sparingly; if more than one dash appears in a sentence, then two dashes — used as a pair to separate an idea — are the limit.)

"He took a stand . . . . albeit a weak stand." (In American English, the use of the ellipsis should be limited to three periods within a sentence, four to end a sentence.)

"She said they met in New York (in a hospital there.)" (This sentence ends improperly; unless an entire sentence is in parentheses, move the period outside the parentheses and before the close of the quotation marks.)

"No more should the individual be expecting handouts from the government". (The practice in American usage is to place the final period inside the quotation marks; in British English, the period falls outside.)

"Would you like to know the results of your examination"? (Again, American usage places the final mark, even a question mark, inside the quotation if the entire sentence is a question; notice the difference in a question that contains only a partial quotation: "What is in the file marked 'personal'?")

"The four-year old product lacked promotion and was soon dropped from the market." (Once hyphens are used in a modifier, they should be used throughout, as in "four-year-old product.")

"I completely disagree with the conclusions from your experiment!." (Some writers are tempted to double the end punctuation when an exclamation point or a question mark is used; those marks, however, end the sentence, and no period should be added.)

"The automobiles differed considerably in one aspect during their road tests; acceleration." (An example or an explanation should be separated from the main part of the sentence by a colon; save the semicolon to separate the main sentence into two or more equal clauses, as it appears in this sentence.)

"Their purpose in the experiment is: to discover how fast water is absorbed." (Even though a colon may introduce an explanation, use the mark only when necessary; it is not needed after a verb, and here the sentence is clearer without the punctuation.)

"He turned down the invitation for dinner because he dislikes the Johnsons cooking." (An apostrophe is needed in "the Johnsons' cooking" — unless he dislikes the Johnsons themselves when they cook instead of disliking their cooking.)

"The generator's will be available by next Tuesday." (*Generators* is the proper plural, and the apostrophe makes a word possessive, not plural.)

"Next Wednesday [the 15th will be soon enough to complete the project." (Always remember that brackets or parentheses must be used in pairs; once the opening mark is used, the closing mark must follow, turning "Wednesday [the 15th will" into "Wednesday [the 15th] will. . . .")

"No pipes or cigars please." (Without punctuation, these words suggest that pipes and cigars do not please; separate the *please* from the rest of this sentence fragment with a comma.)

21

SPEAKING

THE POWERS OF SPEECH

HAMLET APPROACHES his band of players before a rehearsal to offer some theatrical advice. "Speak the speech," he tells them, "as I pronounced it to you, trippingly on the tongue." Although such lingual dexterity is rare these days, the advice still works in power speaking. Enunciation is as important to speech as spelling is to writing. The keys to power speaking all benefit from Hamlet's sage saying.

"Speech is power," Ralph Waldo Emerson wrote, adding, "Speech is to persuade, to convert, to compel." The primary advice to any speechmaker boils down to the three-part wisdom of advertising: "Tell 'em what you're gonna tell 'em. Then tell 'em. Then tell 'em what you told 'em." That triple threat of a message serves to reinforce the meaning and keep the departing audience from wondering what the speech was about. Combining that advice with the four keys to power speaking will advance any spoken message.

SPEAK TO A LISTENER

When Winston Churchill found a big crowd waiting to hear him lecture, he remained composed. "I always remember," he said, "that if instead of making a political speech, I was being hanged, the crowd would be twice as big."

The same way that a writer needs to envision a reader, every speaker should try to speak to a listener. Sometimes when a message is recorded or a broadcast is made, no listener is present, but the speaker may still visualize such a person. The debilitating fear of public speaking can be overcome by that image. The friendlier the response of the imagined listener, the more confident the speaker becomes, and the main element of that confidence is preparation.

Rehearse the planned message at least three times before any major speech and the words will come more naturally; less rehearsal may lead to reading the speech, as though the words were committed to paper for fear of not being committed to memory. A simple exercise is to set aside the notes and recite the main points of the speech without being cued or coached. With practice, even the most reluctant public speaker can make what seems like dreadful anticipation turn into sudden calm.

"HASTEN THY STORY"

The imperative message, an Eleventh Commandment, is posted prominently in a newspaper bureau: "Hasten thy story."

Speakers should take a hint from it. As far back as the New Testament, the advice was given: "Be quick to listen and slow to speak." Even a speech that starts well will leave a bitter feeling if it continues too long or strays too far from the point. Anything that moves away from the speaker's point should be considered filler and removed as quickly as possible. Only the material that moves the point along should remain.

Visualizing that potential listener — or practicing before an actual listener — may help, particularly when the talk produces expressions of puzzlement or boredom. Confusion results whenever the argument or explanation needs to be sharpened, and tiredness occurs when the talk grows weary. Take cues from the listener and shape the speech accordingly.

Even in formal speeches, converse with the audience as much as possible. It is the difference between *talk to,* which is for lecturing, and *talk with,* which is for conversing. At the same time, limit the *um* and *ah* and *er* and *well* that undercut communication, and offer a message full of meaning, not filler.

Hasten the story to the earliest possible conclusion. Demosthenes may have had the oratorical power to keep an audience spellbound for hours, but most speakers will never face an audience of ancient Greeks.

"SUIT THE ACTION TO THE WORD"

Hamlet's advice to the players continues. Waving his hand, he tells them, "Nor do not saw the air too much with your hand, thus," adding, "Suit the action to the word, the word to the action."

A soap opera character telephones his newest girlfriend. "I think there's a whole lot to be said for eye contact, body language," he says. "You can learn a whole lot by being in the same room with someone." Here the speaker has the advantage over the writer. Body language allows all sorts of meanings to be added to the words, from gestures to facial expressions.

Power language is more than words can say, and gestures can make all the difference. Ham actors know how to prolong an audience's response by saying "No! No!" while waving for more applause, with as much sincerity as if they had said, "Stop it some more." A gesture can easily upstage a word.

Make sure, though, that the gesture is appropriate to the word. Gestures and positions taken together have formed their own category of body language, and the physical comments may often say more than the mere words. Listeners who say, "Yes, I believe you," while shaking their heads may not be so trusting as their words imply. A similar error occurs during a dramatic scene; two young actresses play sisters discussing their family, and while one speaks, the other fidgets, waving her right hand repeatedly and drawing the attention entirely from the words. Afterward, the director explains the mistake, telling the more active actress, "I kept expecting you to do something — pull out a gun or a knife — and it caused a lot of lines to slip away." Suit every action to the word, adding no extraneous actions, and the word is strengthened.

Speakers must also be prepared for gestures by the listeners. Audience members often yawn — a reflex to help stay awake — but the person talking may be disconcerted by seeing too many yawns. Some lecturers prefer not to see the audience, and they may use visual aids such as slides to avoid direct eye contact. Others know how to deal with everything from hecklers to crying babies by drawing them into the topic at hand; a minister stops in the midst of a baptism service when the baby begins to cry: "Praise the Lord," she says, "we'll have another member for the choir."

PRONOUNCE PROPERLY AND CLEARLY

"We help injured people," the announcer says in a television commercial for an insurance agency. The final letter on *injured*, however, is sometimes swallowed, and "We help injure people" sounds like a commercial for a gang of thugs. Saying what is meant requires that the talk be understood, and the sole responsibility for enunciation falls on the speaker.

Words must be pronounced properly, and any good dictionary can give the proper sounds and the syllables to emphasize. Defense is not "*dee*-fense," nor is insurance "*in*-sur-ance." Both *February* and *library* have an *r* after the *b*, and *deteriorate* and *subsidiary* have more syllables than are often pronounced. The term *juxtaposed* should not come out as *juxtasposed*; no extra sounds are necessary. Neither should syllables be added ("ath-uh-lete" is a mistake for *athlete*) or subtracted ("pol-ih-cal" for *political*). Although purists may still argue, a shift in stress to the second syllable has overtaken such pronunciations as "*lam*-entable," "*hos*-pitable," "*des*-picable." The incorrect *gonna* is not "going to"; *ax* is not "ask," *ek setera* not "et cetera."

Although the final letter often falls off words ending in -*ing*, the speaker should make the effort to be understood. When a flat statement is being made, for example, no invisible question marks should raise declarative sentences into the realm of questions. Speaking well requires a physical effort far different from the act of writing, and speakers who fail to make themselves heard may find their speeches poorly received.

Precise pronunciation should accompany concise wording. A motivational speaker on network television uses "basically," "I mean," and "you know" in various combinations throughout his talk, turning off the audience. Anybody who says, "This is the main, you know, point" has little hope of power language.

Nervousness often accounts for lost power in speaking. An Associated Press report tells how one businesswoman calmed her fears of speaking in front of Governor Mario Cuomo of New York. After her talk, she told the governor, "I've been imagining you naked." Other tricks of speaking include the practice of slowing down deliberately, the well-timed pause, the louder voicing of important ideas, and especially the direct address of the listeners. Use each of these tricks wisely and well to empower speech.

Several reminders, drawn from an informal poll of lecturers and speech teachers, should also help the speaker:

- Be animated but not manic.
- Breathe deeply to overcome nervousness.
- Have the first and last sentences memorized.
- Maintain eye contact with members of the audience as much as possible.

- Practice enough, but remember that too much rehearsal makes talking sound like lecturing.

A professional speaker adds, "A genuine smile cannot hurt, and always remember the power of positivity." Peggy Noonan, the former White House speechwriter, made the same point, noting on speechmaking that the positive "always remember" is far more effective than the negative "never forget" in moving an audience.

As the speech nears its end, speakers often want to emphasize certain words of the message. In the same way a singer slows the tempo and extends the notes to end a song, the speaker may want to slow and stress the message.

Always remember, though, not to read to an audience. Nothing is worse than the speaker, staring intently at handheld index cards, who begins, "I am your [next card] speaker. My name is [next card] John."

Power speakers must also guard against the misheard word. Forty years ago, the writer Sylvia Wright coined a term for these sound misunderstandings: mondegreens. She took the word from her own example of such an error; when a Scottish poem was recited about a hero's treatment after his death (they "laid him on the green"), she misheard the phrase as "Lady Mondegreen."

The labeling of mondegreens led to a flood of similarly misheard phrases, from the Pledge of Allegiance ("I pled a legion to the flag") to the Christmas carol "Hark! the Herald Angels Sing" (leading children to ask which angel is named Harold) and even Handel's *Messiah* (with "reign" misheard as a weather report: "And He shall rain forever and ever"). The name of the Empire State Building has been twisted from "the Empire Steak Building" to the "Entire Ache Building," and viewers of the film *Airplane!* recall the exasperated response of the pilot when he hears sentences that begin with *surely:* "And stop calling me Shirley!" Rock music has produced numerous mondegreens, including the song "Lucy in the Sky with Diamonds" (a Beatles hit misheard as "Lucy in Disguise with Diamonds") and the duo Hall and Oates (mistakenly heard by some as "haulin' oats").

Among literary mondegreens, perhaps the most endearing appears in the 1944 Tennessee Williams play *The Glass Menagerie,* when the painfully shy Laura Wingfield tells of her nickname in high school. After a severe bout of pleurosis, she returned to school and told her classmate Jim why she had been absent. He misunderstood *pleurosis,* though, and began to call her "Blue Roses."

Few misheard words are that poetic, however. Instead, they tend to embarrass the speaker or at least slow the flow of communication (diners may hear "Super salad?" when the waiter asks, "Soup or salad?"). Here are ten mondegreens, from television promotions and newspaper reports, along with the proper wording that has gone astray.

THE WORD MISHEARD

"Do you have a cute back pain?" (This television ad was trying to inquire about *acute* back pain.)

"To itch his own." (An attempt to pronounce the saying "To each his own" failed to sound the long *e* that begins *each.*)

"Makes snails stronger." (The commercial for a fingernail product needed a clearer separation of words to sound out "Makes nails stronger.")

"I drive a cabin-banger." (An unfamiliar vehicle, *cabin-banger* turned out to be the territory of a Maine taxi driver: "a cab in Bangor.")

"Throughout the interview the press was offered a performance of can-dancers." (Again, elision causes confusion that may be cleared up by separating *can-dancers* into *canned answers.*)

"Be careful to read the instructions before operating this forehead VCR." (The machine does not balance on the forehead; instead, it is a *four-head VCR.*)

"See our new thirty-second animated feature." (What sounds like an extremely brief film is actually an impressive achievement: the studio's successor to its thirty-first animated feature.)

"I can understand what you have been through with your child, because I'm apparent too." (Understanding is even clearer when *apparent* is separated into *a parent.*)

"He looks like a deer caught in head lice." (Few deer have been caught in *head lice;* the surprised expression is meant to imitate the look of a deer caught in *headlights.*)

"The average American will gain forty-seven pounds during the holidays." (This frightening statistic loses most of its weight when interpreted correctly: "gain *four to seven* pounds.")

IV

POWER SECRETS

HOW TO WIN WITH WORDS

22

ALLITERATION

SOUND EXERCISE

POETS AND PROSE WRITERS alike have found comfort and capability in a select secret or two for wording power. Not well kept but well established, these power secrets allow words to work well together. The first of these secrets elicits power from sound.

"Peter Piper picked a peck of pickled peppers" and similar sayings have provided amusement and amazement when spoken quickly. These tongue twisters also illustrate the power of sounds and their inherent force when combined.

Capturing some of that force is possible when words are handled carefully. The first secret requires taking seriously what may seem like the silliness of childhood word games. Once the secret of alliteration is practiced, the word user has an advantage previously limited mainly to politicians and advertising copywriters.

LISTEN WELL

Just as a speaker needs a good listener, every speaker and writer should be a good listener.

Listening well is not an innate skill. A good listener pays attention to the words offered, makes mental notes of the important words, and responds in a way that will help the communication continue: "I can hear your pain," a therapist tells each of her patients. Failing to listen well, however, will result not only in losing the other person's attention but also in finding that attention much harder to gain the next time.

Perhaps the best result from power listening is the ability to use the other person's words to advantage. Debaters excel at using an opponent's word in opposing. "I think it's disgraceful," one debater will say, and the effective rebuttal begins, "What would be more disgraceful is. . . ." Catching the other person off guard provides extra power. In the nineteenth century, when the critic Margaret Fuller was reported to have said, "I accept the universe," the British essayist Thomas Carlyle framed the obvious response to such an immodest proposal: "By God! she'd better." Today's critics are also adept at turning a word or title back on itself. A film sequel drew a negative review from *Variety*, whose critic wrote, "*The Neverending Story* lives up to its title in the worst way possible."

Proper listening adds force to a message by hearing certain repeated sounds in deliberate patterns. The good reader, like a listener, "hears" the words while reading and catches the same nuances of sounds. To work toward better listening, practice hearing the sounds of words.

SOUND OUT WORDS

In Neil Simon's comedy *The Sunshine Boys*, a retired comic tries to explain what causes humor. "Words with a *k* in it are funny," he says, offering such examples as "car keys," "pickle," and "Cleveland."

For these power secrets to work, word users need to work on their sensitivity to the sounds of words. Words may be linked by similar sounds and separated by differing sounds. The ability to recognize similar sounds will lead to an ability to use those sounds to advantage.

Notice the difference in sound between calling an idea *wrong* and calling it *fallacious.* Beyond the more sophisticated (or pretentious) sound of the second word, its sound allows pairing with other words that *wrong* would weakly join. "Fallacious phrase," for example, has a euphony that is absent in "wrong phrase."

SET SIMILAR SOUNDS SIDE BY SIDE (SOMETIMES)

Three sound patterns are practiced regularly by public speakers and advertisers. Each has its own force and, in varied combination, each may keep an audience carefully tuned to the message.

First comes alliteration. This pattern relies on opening sounds, whether consonant or vowel, repeated to link words that begin similarly. It invokes the force of sound, from the children's game of *Where's Waldo?* to the John Steinbeck novel *East of Eden.* On the news show *60 Minutes,* a federal inspector from an academic background is identified as "a bookworm with a badge." Top students are known as "the best and the brightest," and the entry to a Philadelphia train station offers the advice "Listen! Look! Live!"

Too much alliteration in a short time can sound comical and keep the message from being taken seriously. Children's books often thrive on alliteration, but the adult ear revels in some similarity and rebels at too much of that good thing. Training the ear to hear and use alliteration also requires training the ear not to abuse the pattern. Two or three words may well be linked by alliteration; more than three words, however, will begin to sound forced or strained.

Next is consonance. This device plays only on consonant

sounds and their repetition in close proximity. No longer do the sounds have to begin the words so long as the repetition is soon enough to notice the connection. Watch the letters *s* and *w*, for example, in *How the West Was Won* for the effect of consonance, similar to the repeated consonant sounds in *The Red Badge of Courage*. An essay on moviegoers faced with too many film choices uses the phrase "multiplex complex," relying again on consonance for effect. With the flow of repeated consonants, viewers of a late-evening news show are advised, "Before you turn in, tune in."

Third, and perhaps more subtle than the others, is assonance. This repetition of vowel sounds links words less obviously, but it can keep the listener's attention focused. The long *e* in "We the people" provides that lift at the start of the Constitution. Radio offers "golden oldies" ("a blast from the past"), including the assonance of the repeated vowel sound in "Blue Moon."

Watch the overuse and abuse of this key. As mondegreens show, similar sounds in words may cause problems in processing the message. The errors increase as the spoken word is translated into print. Homophones — words that sound the same but have different meanings and often different spellings — lead to serious errors in transmitting the message.

Following are thirty-five frequent homophone mistakes, each followed by its correct form. Sound is important, but unless sense joins with sound, the message may be lost.

HOMOPHONE CALLS

"The speaker at the annual meeting was a little horse." (This report proved far less exciting than it sounded; the speaker, having throat trouble, was only a little *hoarse.*)

"Let's raise the level of our thinking and promote plane speaking." (Unless the discussion is about aircraft, the speaking should be *plain.*)

"We reported the principle findings of the committee." (Those main findings are *principal*, unless they covered values or basic beliefs.)

"Candidate Stood on Principal." (The headline of this newspaper article was not accompanied by a picture of a candidate atop a school leader; here the proper spelling would be *principle*.)

"Coral Call to Worship." (This phrase in a church bulletin should have used *choral*, as in "of a choir.")

"Readers have been pouring over the small print." (Another reader may wonder what they have been *pouring*; careful reading or study is *poring*.)

"Still searching for the missing worker, they tried to canvas the area before the storm." (It would be difficult to cover a large area with canvas; the searchers were trying to *canvass* the area.)

"We played at parties and showers to make ends meat." (Nobody tries to make ends *meat*; the proper verb here is *meet*.)

"It's quite a plumb — I'm sure there isn't another city that wouldn't want this project." (Perhaps this rewarding project is a *plum*; plumbing is the work of a plumber.)

"They asked the actor weather he ever ad-libs his lines." (Expect a stormy response to this misuse of *weather*; for a choice, the term is *whether*.)

"Make a right turn by the loan oak." (A tree that stands by itself is a *lone* oak.)

"Now we gather on the same sight to celebrate its history." (All may see the same *sight*, but they must be gathered on the same location or *site*.)

"Trying to diffuse the hostile situation, the leaders met in secrecy." (A situation that may blow up needs somebody to *defuse* it; *diffuse* means "to spread or scatter.")

"White wine compliments the chicken dinner." (Unless the wine flatters the chicken, it merely *complements*, by completing or making perfect; if the meal is perfect, the chef deserves *compliments*.)

"He stepped over the fowl line before he threw the ball." (No chicken drew a *fowl* line; the boundary line separates fair and *foul* territory.)

"Garages provide unlikely hangers for planes." (This newspaper report suggests that airplanes should be suspended on *hangers*; the place for parking a plane is a *hangar*.)

"You must move rapidly to staunch a hemorrhaging budget." (The financial officer should move rapidly to replace *staunch*, an adjective for "steadfast," with the proper verb *stanch*, which means "to stop the flow of.")

"Exercise your vocal chords before the concert." (The voice has no *chords*, which are groups of musical notes played together; instead, use vocal *cords*.)

"In its hayday, the company was increasing its profits every year." (Unless the company devotes a day to selling hay, the proper term for success is *heyday*.)

"The cookwear should be polished until it shines." (*Cookwear* is perhaps something a chef would dress in; the pots and pans are *cookware*.)

"Several players have been placed on wavers this season." (A *waver* is somebody who waves or signals; players who have been dropped from the roster were put on *waivers*.)

"The taught bands squeezed into his wrists." (A *taught* band may be an educated musical group; bands that squeeze should be *taut*.)

"Tax employees were accused of peaking at the returns of friends and relatives." (*Peak* means "to reach the heights"; the verb for a furtive look is *peek*, and any misuse of that term may cause pique.)

"The sense of rosemary and thyme filled the kitchen." (With the sense of smell, a cook may detect the *scents* of those herbs.)

"In the final scene, the villain received his just desserts." (Unless the villain was served cake and ice cream, he probably received his punishment, known as just *deserts*.)

"The demolition company plans to raise the old building next week." (No old building was being lifted; instead, to demolish a building is to *raze* it.)

"We trust that you will be discrete with this information." (The adjective *discrete* means "separate, apart"; here the word should be *discreet*, as in "able to keep a secret.")

"Envelopes may be found in the stationary aisle." (This store direction seems to suggest that other aisles will be moving; *stationary* should be replaced with *stationery* for letters and envelopes.)

"Patch the trouble spot with as much duck tape as possible." (The product is *duct* tape, not *duck.*)

"The chef has a flare for difficult dishes." (Unless the dishes are being flame-cooked, the proper noun is *flair*, meaning "style," not a *flare*, as in a burning signal.)

"Consumers report duel problems with the new equipment." (Two opponents may undertake a *duel*, but the simple adjective for "two-part" is *dual.*)

"Forego the costs of updating the system until it becomes necessary." (To do without is to *forgo*; with an *e*, the verb *forego* means "to precede, go before.")

"The imminent lawyer has won hundreds of cases." (Such a lawyer would be *eminent*, meaning "famous"; pronounced with a slight difference, *imminent* means "about to happen.")

"Lower wage earners have born most of the expense so far." (*Born* means "given birth"; the term for "carried" is *borne.*)

"Expect increases in the bus fair next month." (This announcement should have used the word *fare* for "cost," because the increase may or may not be *fair.*)

23

RHYME AND RHYTHM

MOTION IN POETRY

RHYMES AND RHYTHMS put the music into words. From ancient poets to modern rappers, word users have known the power of rhyme to make words more pleasing, more euphonious. Rhyme especially has the ability to move a passage along, making strong words stronger and more memorable. Rhythm also adds to the musical quality of the words, providing a back-beat of sound patterns to propel the words. Recognizing rhyme and rhythm and using them to advantage are important in working with language.

RHYME CAREFULLY

The soothing sound of rhyming words adds a musical, lilting quality not otherwise found in language. To harness that quality, the writer or speaker needs to know the types of rhyme available, creating combinations of words or sounds that have turned a basketball franchise into a "dream team" or a volume of recipes into a "cookbook."

Exact rhyme works best. This form connects two strong syllables that begin with different sounds and end with the same vowel and consonant sounds. *Dream* and *team* form such a bond, and *no pain, no gain* has pushed many an athlete to the limit.

Rhyme aids memory. When the lawyer Alan M. Dershowitz wanted a memorable title for his book on legal tactics for avoiding blame, he chose *The Abuse Excuse.* Similarly, cookies by somebody named just Amos might have tasted as good, but the chocolate chip empire came from "Famous Amos," just as a laundry product uses rhyme in "When a light scent is the right scent."

Ann Landers also uses rhyme, advising an insensitive correspondent, "I think you need a checkup from the neck up." A psychic healer on TV tells about "an essential part of the healer's art," and the country singer Crystal Gayle performs, "There's nothing colder than your old cold shoulder." Tablets to fight indigestion are "made stronger to last longer"; a prepared lunch is "complete and fun to eat," and a new perfume is "the spray lingerie."

The ultimate rhyming ad may be for the Boot Hill Saloon, advertised as "across from the cemetery" in Daytona Beach, Florida. Its motto: "Order a drink and have a seat. You're better off here than across the street."

Less forceful than exact rhyme is sight rhyme, when two or more words appear to the eye to rhyme but are exposed by the ear not to rhyme. *Love* and *move,* once rhyming words in English, have had enough change in vowel sounds that they now appear to rhyme but do not.

Next comes near rhyme, a combining of consonance and assonance to link two words that almost rhyme. Song lyrics are full of these near rhymes, words such as *fine* and *time.*

In poetry, end rhyme marks the placement of the rhyming words at the end of each line. Prose writers and speakers are less concerned with having the end of one sentence rhyme with the end of the next, but the occasional insertion of rhyming words does move prose along.

Rhyme also works within a line. Robert Browning's "Confessions" offers this line: "How sad and bad and mad it was." A popular entertainer uses a rhyme if he forgets a name; he tells the person, "I can't place your face."

Rhyming words can also lead to effective spoonerisms. Named for the British clergyman William Spooner, these wordplays come from reversing the initial consonant sounds ("tons of soil" for "sons of toil"). A display of gardening books offers this spoonerism based on the poker cliché of "Read 'em and weep": "Weed 'em and reap!"

The user of power language should use rhyme sparingly, never confusing slang words that rhyme and "rhyming slang." That specific category of linguistic folklore does not cover such rhymes as "Keep your eyes on the prize"; it refers to avoiding the naming of something by using a rhyming term (saying "plates of meat" instead of "feet"), a linguistic game favored in Cockney speech.

Also, use reduplications rarely. Words such as *booboo* and *bye-bye* began by duplicating the first syllable into a two-part term. Less exact duplications reached for rhyming rather than repeated syllables: *hanky-panky* and *willy-nilly*. These terms have built-in rhyme and, used too often, sound like children's singsong verse rather than serious prose.

ADD RHYTHM CONSCIOUSLY

Words form a natural fall and rise as they are joined in phrases and clauses. The aware writer or speaker can occasionally use the rhythms of words to emphasize the message. Most often, these patterns help in titles or names.

In professional sports, for example, rhythm patterns recur in the names of teams. Five primary forms of rhythm are found in the use of accented and unaccented syllables.

1. Iambic rhythm offers the Shakespearean beat of an unaccented syllable followed by an accented one: "To *be* or *not*

to *be.*" Major league baseball teams with that same name rhythm include Atlanta Braves and Chicago Cubs.

2. Trochaic rhythm, as in *The Raven,* reverses that pattern, starting on the accent and following it without an accent ("*Once* up-*on* a *mid*-night *drear*-y"). Trochees rebound in names of basketball teams: Boston Celtics, Charlotte Hornets, Houston Rockets.

3. Anapestic rhythm builds from two unaccented syllables (one more than iambic) to a strong syllable, as in "'Twas the *night* before *Christ*-mas and *all* through the *house.* . . ." Listen for anapests in the names of Philly's finest: Philadelphia Flyers, Philadelphia Seventy-sixers, Philadelphia Eagles.

4. Dactylic rhythm starts with a strong syllable, followed by two unaccented syllables (one more than trochaic), the beat heard in "*dac*-tyls and *an*-a-pests." Hockey fans hear dactyls in their teams: Ottawa Senators and Washington Capitals.

5. Spondaic rhythm pushes two equally strong syllables together, as in "*two e*-qual-ly *strong syl*-la-bles." Michigan fans spot spondees in Detroit Tigers, Detroit Pistons, Detroit Red Wings, and Detroit Lions.

These rhythms and various syncopations can power the prose. Knowing combinations of these rhythms can provide the energy to propel phrases and clauses.

TRY POETIC DEVICES OCCASIONALLY

Figures of speech should occasionally figure in speech and writing. The key word is "occasionally," because the overuse of any of the following makes words sound overworked. Slip in a simile or perhaps personification rarely, and weak words may gain power.

1. Simile. A comparison of unlike things is made with *as* or *like.* From the Robert Burns line "O, my Luve is like a red, red rose" to Madonna's "Like a Virgin," the simile provides a comparison for the audience to understand.

2. Metaphor. More direct than a simile, this figurative language makes the connection between unlike things without using *like* or *as*. The Greek playwright Sophocles introduced the "ship of state" metaphor; modern metaphor reaches into comic strips, where Charles M. Schulz points out in *Peanuts* that "Happiness is a warm puppy."
3. Personification. This figure gives human traits to something nonhuman. From the "weeping willow" to a "laughing hyena," personification is the personal touch.
4. Metonymy. A person or thing is identified by something closely associated with that person or thing. Using *the crown* for a king or queen is one example and calling reporters *pencils* another.
5. Synecdoche. Here the person or thing is identified by a part. A car takes the slang name of *wheels*; a working sailor is a *hand* ("All hands on deck!").
6. Foreshadowing. This literary technique signals early in the work what will come later. In *Oedipus Rex*, Sophocles introduces a blind truthsayer, who foreshadows the fate of Oedipus by the end of the play. By dropping hints, a writer or speaker may create suspense.
7. Syllepsis. Through shortened syntax, this figure allows a word used in more than one sense to surprise the audience. On *Roseanne*, the title character is asked whether she worked "on a computer" at her last job; she replies, "No, I worked on my feet." Arriving home late, Roseanne asks her daughter if she had put her little brother to sleep, and the daughter says dryly, "I didn't know I had that option."

Carelessly chosen words can throw off the rhythm of the sentence, and the meaning may be buried if the words have more than one sense. Telephone pranks rely on these two-way words in impish questions such as "Is your refrigerator running?" or "Do you have Prince Albert in the can?" Readers of Clement Moore's *Visit from Saint Nicholas* may find that "tore open the shutters and threw up the sash" leaves them feeling queasy.

In finding ways to emphasize words, the writer or speaker needs to select powerful words to hold strong positions. Expressions with more than one sense tend to slow the message. A loan company, for example, promises "Questionable Credit!" There may well be uncertainty about whether the phrase fits the company or the customer. Similarly, the word *auditor* has two senses; in "He was frightened by the auditors," the subject may fear public speaking or tax audits.

The following examples show two-way words and phrases, weakened by double meanings.

TWO-TIMING TERMS

WORDS

APPEALING: "The defense attorney in this case is appealing." (The word may mean either "attractive" or "seeking a review.")

DROP: "Don't forget to drop your pants at the cleaners." (This instruction forgets that the verb can mean "leave" or "lower.")

GOOD: "He wants to be a political force for good." (He wants the job to be either "charitable" or "permanent.")

OUTGOING: "I can't remember when the outgoing service ended." (This adjective may mean either "friendly" or "headed outward.")

PRESENTLY: "She's going to call her sister presently." (This two-way word may mean "now" or "soon.")

PRODUCTIVE: "The company doctor checked any worker with a cough that's productive." (The company would prefer that the worker, not the cough, be "productive.")

RECALL: "It's always a hasty word you can't recall." (Remember that this verb has two meanings: "to remember" or "to cause to return.")

REVOLTING: "We've decided that we're revolting." (This word can signal either a revolution or disgust.)

RICH: "The leader of that group is certainly rich." (Take this adjective to mean either "wealthy" or "laughable.")

SANGUINE: "Their sanguine meeting attracted the world's attention." (This old word has one sense of "cheerful," another of "bloody.")

SWIPE: "Please swipe credit card." (As an instruction on gas pumps, this phrase forgets the double sense of the slang *swipe:* "to slide" or "to steal.")

THOUGHTFUL: "You seem awfully thoughtful today." (Another two-way adjective, *thoughtful* may mean "considerate" or "worried.")

PHRASES

ALL OVER: "The news about the plane crash is all over." (This phrase — which also occurs in the newspaper riddle "What's black and white and read all over?" — mixes the senses of "everywhere" and "finished.")

CARRY ON: "They expected the speaker to carry on for another hour." (In speaking, *carry on* may mean either "to continue" or "to ramble.")

CHRISTMAS PRESENTS: "Christmas Presents Mixed Bag." (This newspaper headline may be read with "Christmas presents" as a noun phrase for "gifts" or, with a different pronunciation, as a clause for "Christmas provides.")

GO BY: "The cab driver chose to go by the location of the next call." (The verb phrase *go by* means either "to pass next to" or "to stop at"; the difference will be significant to the person who called for the taxi.)

HANG WITH: "Hang backstage with your favorite stars." (With the vogue of dropping prepositions, "hang out with" became "hang with," having dual senses of "spend time with" or "dangle from a rope with.")

HOLD UP: "Our delivery man was held up on his way to the store." (*Hold up* may mean either "to delay" or "to rob.")

OUTDOOR WRITER: "He has gained fame as an outdoor writer." (Either he works outside or he writes about the great outdoors.)

SELL OUT: "We are all familiar with performers who have succeeded in selling out." (This verb phrase may have the positive sense of "to sell all the tickets" or the negative sense of "to compromise for money.")

TAKE IN: "Others who have been taken in will also be surveyed." (The double sense of this phrase is "treat well" or "cheat well.")

TAKE OUT: "The agent decided to take out the spy he had befriended." (This term has a friendly meaning of "to date" and a fiendish meaning of "to kill.")

TURN ON: "By the end of the evening, the two began to turn on each other." (As a verb phrase, *turn on* may mean "to excite," but it also means "to become hostile.")

WEAR OUT: "She wasn't supposed to wear it out." (This verb phrase has the double sense of "to display" or "to ruin by prolonged use.")

24

EMPHASIS

STRESS FOR SUCCESS

TENNESSEE WILLIAMS BOASTED of his ability to clear a room with just two words. His audience, waiting for him to continue, was startled by the playwright's sudden cry of "Fire! Fire!"

Repetition offers dramatic power. "Are you talking to me?" Robert De Niro's shady character asks in the film *Taxi Driver*. He repeats the question, with even more stress, as a challenge: "Are *you* talking to *me*?"

Stress tests, used to determine the human capacity for handling pressure, may also help to determine the language's capacity for power. The stress factor in language indicates the ability to emphasize and accent words based on their force and their position. Finding patterns that build power and eliminating those that remove strength can provide a significant assist to winning words. Through four keys, the use of stress or emphasis allows words to stand out and underscore the message.

STRESS SPECIFIC WORDS

The eager student begins to mark the important passages in the reading material with a highlighter pen, and the finished product may soon be a solid page of highlighting. The importance of emphasis begins with a recognition of what material needs to be stressed. Stressing everything is another way of stressing nothing.

Knowing the message to be communicated is necessary for proper emphasis. From that message, the terms worthy of highlighting become apparent as the words most likely to help communicate the meaning. Finding these words and using strategies to stress the most important terms will send that message to its receivers with the most efficiency.

In the effort to add stress, be careful about the dishonest language of overstating or understating. An example of an overstated introduction is "the legendary celebrity psychic." Advertising and book blurbs are often written in excessive superlatives, perhaps none more overstated than this puff: "As a universally known poet, he writes the most beautiful poems of all times." (The work is not by Shakespeare or Sylvia Plath but by a poet in Indiana.)

Hyperbole takes many forms, as in Al Jolson's offer in "My Mammy" to walk a million miles for a smile. A talk show host turns to her guest and says, "Tell us about the day that ripped your life apart." Perhaps Superman should be held responsible for the raising of every performer to *superstar,* every model to *supermodel.* The lowly *party animal* is elevated to *party god,* and the prefix *mega-* rules (a senator referred to a bill in Congress as a "mega-turkey"). To overstate is to sledgehammer home the point.

Handled wisely, understatement can be much more effective, giving the writer or speaker an edge with a hedge. "We didn't exactly hit it off," says one mortal enemy of another. A wife donates a kidney to her husband and says, "It was a little bit of a struggle, but now everything is all right." Many years ago, when Eddie Cantor introduced Deanna Durbin before her stardom, he said simply, "Here's a thirteen-year-old girl with a nice voice. I think you might like her"; by not even giving a name, he added the power of understatement to her introduction. Recently, the country singer Joe Diffie referred to Earth in a hit song as "Third Rock from the Sun."

In expressing emotion, less always proves more. "It's hard for me to tell you," says a television father to his son, "just how much you do mean to me." A game show host also uses this technique: "We have a prize so wonderful that I don't have the words in my vocabulary to describe it."

Do not rely on adverbs to do the work of verbs or nouns. *Very* is worked too hard as an emphasizer: "the *very* last minute" or "he was *very* tired" (try *deadline* and *exhausted* in place of those expressions).

When using adverbs, limit the choice to one. Nothing needs to be "absolutely, completely, undeniably, totally" modified.

REPEAT BEGINNINGS OR ENDINGS

Shakespeare pushed repetition to the limit in *King Lear.* In that tragedy, the elderly king realizes in the death of his daughter Cordelia the eternity that separates them; he contemplates the limits of that eternity with a single line: "Never," he says and looks at his daughter's body before quietly repeating, "Never." He stares at the ground and says, "Never." He looks hopelessly to those around him and says, "Never," before looking off into the distance and repeating, "Never."

Shakespeare's plays lack directions for line reading, and that single line for Lear is printed as "Never, never, never, never, never." Five uses of the same word in the same sentence, however, should be recognized as the regal limit for repetition. Saying the same word twice strikes the audience often as unnecessary. Repetition adds emphasis, but it is likely to backfire if not handled with extreme care. Writers for soap operas, for example, tend to overuse repetition at the end of the scene, and actors have long blessed the writers who do not require a dramatic line to be repeated with dramaturgical signification: "I'm the only one who knows . . . the only one who knows."

Remember the power of difference. If repetition is used too often (like the highlighter pen), little stands out. Instead, avoid repetition as much as possible; when the technique does become necessary, that rare example of repetition gains even more power.

Palilogy is the effect of the deliberate repetition of a single word. "I am shocked, shocked," a character in *Casablanca* says, and the narrator of a Dylan Thomas poem exhorts his dying father to "rage, rage against the dying of the light." The singer Jimmy Buffett begins "A Pirate Looks at Forty" by repeating the word *mother* in addressing "Mother Ocean."

A current magazine's advertising repeats a sentence, altering only one word in referring to itself: "It's the one they're talking about. It's the one they're arguing about." A car promotion uses the same technique: "You wouldn't buy a cheap parachute. You wouldn't buy a cheap pacemaker. You wouldn't buy a cheap crash helmet. Let's discuss cars."

Anaphora is the use of repeated beginnings, and nobody used it better than Martin Luther King, Jr., in his speech that introduces idea after idea with "I have a dream." That pattern for echoing the starting words dates back to "Thou shalt" in the Ten Commandments and a familiar passage from Ecclesiastes: "A time to be born, and a time to die. . . ." Similarly, repeated endings provide the rhetorical trick of epistrophe, as in "government of the people, by the people, for the people." Those phrases from the Gettysburg Address use a technique as old as the New Testament; recall Paul's first letter to the Corinthians about love: "Love bears all things, believes all things, hopes all things, endures all things."

Varying amounts of sentences are subject to effective repetition. An entire sentence may be repeated; speakers often quote Robert Frost's repetition of "And miles to go before I sleep." On the television series *Unsolved Mysteries,* a report on the supernatural ended with the sobering statement "We can't say yes, but we can't say no." Midsentence repetition of a single word may add an ominous tone, as Shirley Jackson did when she started and ended a frightening novel, *The Haunting of Hill House,* with the words "Whatever walked there walked alone."

These forms of repetition may be found in combination. Watch the anaphora and palilogy working together, for instance, in this powerful line of dialogue from a television drama: "No matter what you say and no matter what you do, you will never, never be accepted."

ARRANGE WORDS EXACTLY

The most important ideas in a sentence should fall in the main clause of that sentence. To increase a word's power, move it from the relative weakness of an introductory clause or phrase to the three primary points of power in any sentence: the subject, the verb, or the object.

In longer forms, such as essays and speeches, emphasis may take the form of an outline, with the major points set up as numbered terms to emphasize. Even in single sentences, however, emphasis may come with the placement of words. In an ordinary sentence, the two strongest positions are the first word and the last word. Rearranging the sentence to place the major word in either of those positions is bound to increase its power. If the major term falls at the end of the sentence, it may well begin with a prepositional phrase or a dependent clause; then the significant word falls not only into the main clause but also at the final position in the sentence.

Build with phrases and sentences to a strong conclusion. A former First Lady was effectively described in the *Washington*

Post as "delicate to the point of wariness, wary to the point of aloofness, aloof to the point of mystery." Listen to the clauses in Alfred Lord Tennyson's *Idylls of the King:* "The days will grow to weeks, the weeks to months, / The months will add themselves and make the years, / The years will roll into the centuries, / And mine will ever be a name of scorn."

Speakers should also build on what has gone before. Repeating a sentence with a word removed can make a powerful answer. A film about the American Revolution shows one colonist trying to persuade another to return to England. "I am going home," says the first. The second shakes his head and replies, "I am home."

"ACCENTUATE THE POSITIVE"

Perhaps no other advice in writing and speaking is more important. The positive outlook carries strength; the negative implies weakness. The World War II song "Accentuate the Positive" still holds true in using language. Finding ways to make the sentence offer even a negative message in a positive form will add force to the phrasing.

Be upbeat as much as possible, preferring "always remember" to "never forget." A positive spin helps the bad news along, as in the restaurant review that "The food was good, but the service was lacking."

Use only one negative at a time. "She's not helping him by not doing it" is the kind of twisted sentence that makes readers or listeners scowl. On the other hand, the conversational double negative can have almost a poetic quality to it. Consider the title of Maya Angelou's inspiring book *Wouldn't Take Nothing for My Journey Now.*

Fuzziness works against emphasis in speech and writing, and the fuzziest usage around is the addition of what are called weasel words. The term was popularized by Theodore Roosevelt, who derided the use of such language eighty years ago. He offered an example: "You can have 'universal training,' or you can have 'voluntary training,' but when you use the word 'voluntary' to qualify the word 'universal,' you are using a weasel word; it has sucked all the meaning out of 'universal.' The words flatly contradict."

Roosevelt may have taken his lead from a *Century* magazine article in 1900 by Stewart Chaplin. "Weasel words," Chaplin wrote, "are words that suck all the life out of the words next to them, just as a weasel sucks an egg and leaves the shell. If you heft the egg afterward, it's as light as a feather, and not very filling when you're hungry; but a basketful of them would make quite a show, and would bamboozle the unwary."

Here is a basketful of weasel words, bound to bamboozle or at least take the power away from emphasized terms. Frequently these words are used unconsciously, with no intention to deceive, but they still weaken the wording, especially when emphasized by suspicious readers. Mostly modifiers, weasel words are the adjectives and adverbs most unlikely to succeed. A translation into plain English follows each example.

WEASEL WORDS

ACTUAL: "The item pictured is not the actual prize" means "Expect a cheap imitation."

ALMOST: "We have almost used up this year's budget" means "We're already broke."

AND UP: "Everything in the store is priced at $20 and up" means "Spend the entire day trying to find the $20 item."

AS FAR AS I CAN TELL: "As far as I can tell, no laws have been broken" means "Laws have been broken."

BASICALLY: "Our ledgers are basically accurate" means "The books have been cooked."

ESSENTIALLY: "The new policy is essentially the same as the old" means "Watch out for the changes."

FOR THE MOST PART: "The contract is straightforward for the most part" means "Look for the loopholes."

GENERALLY: "I am generally informed about that subject" means "I don't have a clue."

NEARLY: "That school is nearly on your way home" means "Prepare to go out of your way."

OR MORE: "Shop here for one dollar or more per item" means "Be ready to spend more than one dollar an item."

PARTICIPATING: "Special deal at participating restaurants only" means "Not to be found at your local franchise."

PRACTICALLY: "I did not get the job that I was practically promised last week" means "Close counts only in horseshoes and hand grenades."

TO MY CERTAIN KNOWLEDGE: "There have been no improprieties; to my certain knowledge, nothing was done wrong" means "I did my best to ignore everything."

UP TO: "Lose up to ten pounds the first week on this diet" means "Be thankful to lose ten ounces."

USUALLY: "We usually complete our projects on time" means "Expect delays."

VIRTUALLY: "Options for the latest vehicles have been virtually unchanged" means "Make sure the steering wheel is still part of the standard equipment."

25

PARALLELISM

THE BALANCING ACT

A HOUSE OF CARDS must be carefully built. One slip of the hand or one uneven section, and the project will collapse. Users of words in powerful combinations should remember that image.

Just as balanced books will stand in a pile without falling, balanced words can stand together without toppling the meaning. Words in formation develop a specific pattern, and following that pattern is the surest way to achieve parallelism. Unfortunately, the usefulness of parallel structure becomes obvious mainly when a word or phrase fails to achieve that balance. Rewording for parallelism, a fast way to winning words, is the ultimate balancing act.

To achieve balance, however, the writer or speaker must first have a sense of what to look for. Whenever an expression seems incomplete or in need of an addition, a likely problem is a lack of balance, which throws off the rest of the sentence. Following three easy keys should correct any lack of parallel structure in favor of balanced language.

PRODUCE PARALLEL TERMS

As the telephone operator Ernestine, Lily Tomlin used parallelism for humor in the days before the breakup of AT&T. Whatever the caller's complaint, Ernestine had a standard response ready: "We don't care. We don't have to. We're the phone company."

In any list of phrases or clauses, the term that lacks parallelism usually stands out. "His favorite activities are skiing, golfing, and to swim" is clearly out of balance, the final phrase an infinitive that fails to parallel the -*ing* nouns (gerunds) preceding it. Turning that final term into a parallel structure — *swimming* — takes no extra syllables but adds a lot of force to the sentence.

Shakespeare never wrote, "To be or not being." A film is advertised for "the head, the heart, and the funny bone"; that perfect parallelism would be lost if *the* were dropped from any one item in the list. The ear listens for the rhythm of the parallelism, and the failure to meet this expectation may well cause the wording to lose power.

A hair-restoring operation promises, "Every person who comes to our office is treated separately and strictly confidential." In that sentence, the adverb *separately* tries to balance the adjective *confidential,* and the construction collapses. Use *confidentially* as an adverb equal to *separately,* and the force is with the phrase.

Here is the main virtue of an outline. A list of points to be made will quickly reveal whether the points are balanced; expressing the terms in a parallel form may help reveal points that are weaker and should be subordinated rather than treated with equal force.

When President Bill Clinton spoke at the fiftieth anniversary of D-Day, balance and parallelism added dignity to his prose: "They were the fathers we never knew, the uncles we never met, the friends who never returned, the heroes we can never repay."

BALANCE PHRASES AND CLAUSES

"I try to train people," a motivator says, "to be up and how to have more choices in their lives." Those choices, however, should be expressed in a balanced form. Either "how to be up and how to have" or "to be up and to have" would make the motivator's mistake parallel.

The problem often extends to longer forms. Even if the writer or speaker chooses to go against the rules of grammar, the need for parallelism remains. Even incomplete clauses should remain parallel. When a film executive commented on Fred Astaire's first screen test, he showed an eye for parallelism, if not for talent: "Can't act. Can't sing. . . . Can dance a little."

Exact parallelism produces power. Patrick Henry demonstrated its force with "Give me liberty or give me death!" The poet Christina Rossetti, writing of her own death, uses parallelism in a gentler way: "And if thou wilt, remember, / And if thou wilt, forget." Unexpected words at the end of balanced clauses can easily surprise; the historian Thomas Babington Macaulay springs that trap in "The more I read [Socrates], the less I wonder why they poisoned him."

The occasional exception to the parallelism rule can be a clause shortened after a full clause. The Koran's words to unbelievers — "Ye have your religion, and I my religion" — takes fewer words than the exact parallelism of repeating *have,* but dropping the repeated verb makes the sentence stronger and more memorable.

Of course, words are not alone in requiring balance; the ideas should be parallel, too. A bus poster lists reasons for women to stop smoking — it hurts children's lungs, it causes coughs and colds, it smells — and ends with "Of course, smoking can also make your husband die younger." That use of *of course* throws off the pattern of the first reasons.

Even when the wording contains no errors, parallelism can add force to the phrasing. A newspaper report on an unpopular movie stated, "The film opens this week and is closing next week." Made parallel, the verbs require one less word and work together better in "The film opens this week and closes next week."

OFFSET NEGATIVE TERMS

"You can run," warns an avenger, "but you can't hide." Emily Dickinson was far more eloquent in balancing negative and positive terms: "Because I could not stop for Death, He kindly stopped for me."

An even more effective twist on parallelism is the speech-writer's trick of antithesis, the balancing of a positive statement with a negative one. Perhaps the most famous example of this rhetoric belongs to the inaugural words of John F. Kennedy: "Ask not what your country can do for you; ask what you can do for your country." Turning the first clause around on itself makes the reader or listener pay more attention to the words.

"The mind is its own place," Milton wrote," and in itself / Can make a heav'n of hell, a hell of heav'n." That reversal of the final words adds power. In *Julius Caesar*, Mark Antony's use of *not* follows a positive statement: "I come to bury Caesar, not to praise him." Wording that suggests careful planning by the writer or speaker will probably garner more respect from the audience than unplanned comments or words that suggest no forethought.

When the *New York Times* photographer Chester Higgins, Jr., released a book about his African odyssey, he wrote, "We are Africans not because we are born in Africa, but because Africa is born in us." The turning around of negated words makes a forceful tool for the speaker or writer.

Audiences come to language with certain expectations, and parallelism is important for fulfilling them. There is a satisfaction in a balanced form that feels unresolved if not completed. A minister speaks of the movement "from distress and captivity and destruction to peace and freedom." That motion from three objects to two remains incomplete; add "and safety" or whatever third object will complete the idea.

The word user must be careful, though, that parallelism may change the meaning of a word. A shopping mall in Frederick, Maryland, posts a notice about "No soliciting, loitering, or pets"; it would hardly do to make the final term end in -*ing*. Consider the possibilities in parallelism, but monitor the effects of enforcing parallel structure.

Finding the right balance for words is a power that develops with practice. Being able to take a sentence apart for its phrases and clauses will help, but even the novice can hope to spot the problems in the following sentences. Here are a dozen examples of unbalanced words, followed by more powerful parallelism.

OFF BALANCE

"The elderly and poor need our assistance." (There are two groups represented here, made clearer by repeating *the:* "The elderly and the poor. . . .")

"Change is coming and usher in a new order." (The verbs here are not parallel; try "is coming and ushering" or "comes and ushers" or even "comes to usher.")

"They said they had the money and that they would return soon." (The *that* following the *and* requires a parallel *that* after *said:* "They said that they had the money and that they. . . ." Even stronger is the shorter "They said they had the money and would return soon.")

"She not only walks to work but also to school." (What follows *not only* should be parallel to what follows *but also;* use "not only walks to work but also walks to school" or the simpler "walks not only to work but also to school.")

"The cookware is stainless, odorless, tasteless." (Parallelism here trips over a two-way word; *tasteless* can be less than a compliment, and the sentence should be reworked as "The stainless and odorless cookware produces no taste.")

"They attend a school involved in charity work but is still financially successful." (The use of *but is* requires adding earlier words: "a school that is involved in charity work but is still. . . .")

"He hopes to find either a new partner or new investor." (What comes after *either* must be parallel to what follows *or:* "a new partner or *a* new investor.")

"On the way home or going shopping, they often drive by the park." (The first two phrases are not parallel: "Going home or going shopping" is stronger.)

"Choose a book, magazine, or a newspaper to read." (The three items are not parallel; add *a* before *magazine,* or drop the *a* before *newspaper.*)

"Stand in front of or behind the machine when operating." (This instruction lacks parallel positions: "in front or in back of" or simply "before or behind.")

"Both day and nighttime shifts are available." (The wording is not wrong in this classified ad, but a better balance would be reached with "day and night" or "daytime and night-time.")

"As a performer, she's talented, funny, and always entertains." (Here the contraction of "she is" throws off the parallelism; change *entertains* to *entertaining* for just the right balance.)

26

QUOTATIONS

LIFTING AND UPLIFTING

"I HATE QUOTATIONS," Ralph Waldo Emerson said. "Tell me what you know."

This nineteenth-century writer, among the most widely quoted figures in American literature, may have been protesting too much. Taken to an extreme, quoting may be a mannerism that allows the writer or speaker to hide behind the words of others. A college student submitted a forty-page term paper on Tudor drama; the paper contained thirty-eight pages of long quotations, tiring the reader and failing to show enough original thought by the writer.

At least two skills are needed to get energy from quotations. First, the user must be able to discern a strong quotation, one that is well worded and applies to the situation. Second, the user must also be able to work the quotation into the text without being heavy-handed or simply tacking it on as an afterthought.

QUOTE ACCURATELY

Quotation requires word-for-word exactness. What goes inside quotation marks should be exactly right. The speaker who says, "I shall return," should not be quoted as "He said, 'He shall return.'"

Quotations come from a speaker or writer, and the name of that source should not interrupt the flow of the sentence. "The victim was taken, the prosecutors said, for more than a thousand dollars" puts the attribution between the verb *(was taken)* and its preposition *(for)*, a mistake that detracts from conversational style: "The prosecutors said the victim was taken for more than a thousand dollars."

Exactness also requires truth in context as well as in content. A political ad shows a candidate who seems to deny a growing problem when he says, "There's not a crisis." That quotation, however, came from a longer statement on a talk show: "You should not say, 'There's not a crisis.'" Reference books occasionally shorten quotations for easy indexing; one source cites George Orwell's "Clear language is insincerity," but the full wording of that quotation expresses a far different sentiment: "The great enemy of clear language is insincerity."

Similarly unfair is the ad for a restaurant, quoting a review about the "fabulous dishes"; in context, however, the reviewer had said that the restaurant occasionally produced "fabulous dishes," often overcome by everyday fare. Movie ads are notorious for taking bad reviews and turning their phrases, out of context, into raves. A supporting actor's "hilarious" physical comedy does not allow the film itself to be called "hilarious." The television commercial for a recent novel said, "This summer the best thrillers aren't just at the movies"; the same sentence appeared on the screen but without the *just,* implying that movies have none of the best thrillers.

Writers should also be careful about the verb used with a quotation. A network reported that critics "raved that the new show is 'Watchable,'" hardly a *rave.* The danger of matching a verb other than *said* with the quoted sentence was parodied by the writer Ring Lardner: "'Shut up,' he explained."

Full disclosure requires honesty both in words and in intention. Anything less is plagiarism.

CHECK QUOTATIONS

Whenever possible, use more than one source to check authenticity, wording, and circumstances.

"I was born in a house built by my father," a network news anchor quoted from a book by Richard Nixon. The book actually begins, "I was born in a house my father built." In this case, the information is still accurate, although the cadence of the prose changes.

"It has been said" or "as some would say" is a sure sign of a manufactured quotation or information impossible to check. A *Life* magazine article uses this formulation: "A dog, it has been said, is prose. A cat is a poem." A *Washington Post* writer starts an unverified statement about Australian etymology: "It is said that when English settlers first asked the Aborigines about these oddly proportioned beasts, the natives answered 'kangaroo' and the name stuck. But in the Aboriginal dialect, 'kangaroo' meant 'I do not understand you.' From this first miscommunication followed two centuries of others."

Idle identifiers are often useful for setting up positions to attack or defend. Emily Dickinson writes: "A word is dead / When it is said, / Some say," and *some* is immediately contradicted. "Some say the world will end in fire," Robert Frost wrote, balancing it with "Some say in ice."

Sometimes the writer or speaker may not know the exact wording or the name of the speaker. That problem, however, is usually solved by quick research, often requiring only a brief look in *Bartlett's* or *Simpson's Contemporary Quotations.* If the quotation is not listed and the living source denies the words, however, there is always the ploy of "the source denies having said" as a qualifier.

Never lift quotations, though, without trying to indicate the source. Senator Joseph Biden, in the midst of a 1988 presidential campaign, learned the hard way; he was accused of plagiarizing a speech by Neil Kinnock of Britain ("Why am I the first Kinnock in a thousand generations to be able to get to university?"). The senator's words were not exactly the same, but they were close enough in form and content to qualify as plagiarism. That word comes from a Latin term for *net*, and netting another person's words or ideas to present as original will produce charges of plagiarism.

PARAPHRASE TRUTHFULLY

Context overshadows content in the area of paraphrasing. Once a speaker's exact words have been altered or reworked, the new wording is no longer a quotation, and the truthful writer or speaker will signal the change, noting, "As Mark Twain might have said," instead of "In the words of Mark Twain."

The source of the original words should still receive credit, but at the same time the source should be relieved of any possible blame resulting from the changed quotation. Simply giving the person's name and indicating an inexact quote, however, are not enough. The user must remain faithful to the source's intentions as well.

Paraphrases are never exact quotations. A stock market analyst writes, "To paraphrase Mark Twain, 'The reports of the retail sector's death are greatly exaggerated.'" Because the writer is paraphrasing, however, no quotation marks should be used. Twain's actual words, when a newspaper ran his obituary prematurely, were "The report of my death was an exaggeration."

ALLUDE POETICALLY

For the more advanced speaker or writer, the use of quotation may lead to the fine art of allusion. Perfecting the ability to work an allusive phrase or clause skillfully into a passage allows the user to sound authoritative on a subject.

"A rose by any other name would smell as sweet," Shakespeare wrote in *Romeo and Juliet*. The phrase "by any other name" can be added adeptly to any discussion of similarity; for example, a generic drug by any other name works as well (and often costs less). Finding appropriate phrases from literature and history becomes a game worthy of the finest players and adds a dimension of richness to any writing or speaking.

Sometimes an effective reference results from refusing to use the exact words. "You can imagine what she said" or "Never mind what he said" can elicit more reflection from the audience than an exact quotation may provide. The approach makes all the difference.

Everybody creates quotations. Most of our words, however, are pedestrian, unworthy of repetition. Look instead for the memorable turn of phrase or the forceful idea.

Quotations should uplift, not simply lift the words of somebody else; if no uplifting phrase on the topic may be found, at least be sure that the quotation applies to the subject at hand. "It is a good thing for an uneducated man to read books of quotations," Winston Churchill once commented. *"Bartlett's Familiar Quotations* is an admirable work, and I studied it intently. The quotations when engraved upon the memory give you good thoughts. They also make you anxious to read the authors and look for more." That memorable quotation on quotations may well be appropriate to the topic of education, but it would probably be wasted in an article on cooking.

Speakers frequently try to place aural quotation marks around something questionable or disagreeable. This formula of saying "quote, unquote" or fingering quotation marks in the air places suspicion on the term thus singled out, and the user must make sure the suspicion is deserved.

Other problems with quoting are more serious. The seasoned user of quotations knows to check and recheck the information, the context, and the punctuation. The writer or speaker should be embarrassed by making mistakes in borrowed words; such mistakes reflect badly, especially because they devalue the words of another.

Some quotations are used so often incorrectly that the correct words seem wrong. "Blood, sweat and tears" may sound like a Churchill quotation; his exact words in 1940, however, were "I have nothing to offer but blood, toil, tears and sweat." In the examples that follow, the misquotations are identified with their proper wording.

QUOTE, MISQUOTE

"Wherefore art thou, Romeo?" (This line, spoken by Shakespeare's Juliet, seems to ask Romeo's location; however, *wherefore* means "why," and the proper quotation uses no comma: "Wherefore art thou Romeo?" She asks him why he is Romeo and therefore a member of a feuding family.)

"Elementary, my dear Watson." (Sherlock Holmes never spoke this line, at least not in Sir Arthur Conan Doyle's stories; Basil Rathbone introduced the words in a film version, and the saying stuck.)

"Once more into the breach, friends." (Another Shakespearean misquotation, this line tries to replicate the words from *Henry V:* "Once more unto the breach, dear friends.")

"To gild the lily." (Shakespeare never wrote this line; here is the exact wording in *King John:* "to gild refined gold, to paint the lily.")

"On the straight and narrow." (This depiction of the path to virtue — mistaking *straight* for *strait* — conflates two expressions in the New Testament, specifically in Matthew 7:14: "Because strait is the gate, and narrow is the way.")

"Don't give up the ship!" (In 1813, when Captain James Lawrence was fatally wounded on the U.S. frigate *Chesapeake,* he actually said, "Tell the men to fire faster and not to give up the ship; fight her till she sinks.")

"You Tarzan, me Jane." (The 1932 film *Tarzan, the Ape Man* never used this line; instead, Jane tries to make Tarzan understand her name and gives up in exasperation.)

"Play it again, Sam." (Another false film quotation, this line comes from *Casablanca;* what Humphrey Bogart says to Dooley Wilson is "You played it for her; you can play it for me. Play it!")

"Let them eat cake." (Marie Antoinette is usually charged with saying these words of political disregard for the poor; the first citation of this "thoughtless saying of a great princess" appeared in Jean-Jacques Rousseau's 1767 *Confessions,* a few years before Marie Antoinette came to France.)

"It's déjà vu all over again." (Often attributed to Yogi Berra, the Yankee great disclaims it, and the source of the saying is unknown.)

"I cannot tell a lie." (Every child is taught that George Washington said these words after chopping down a cherry tree; unfortunately, they are the words of Mark Twain attributed to Washington and are based on Mason Weems's report in an 1800 biography that Washington said, "I can't tell a lie. I did cut it with my hatchet.")

"Nice guys finish last." (Leo Durocher never spoke these exact words, although the quotation is assigned to him; instead, he did say of the New York Giants, "They're the nicest guys in the world! And where are they? In seventh place!" Sportswriters and editors reformed the comment.)

"Come up and see me sometime." ("Why don't you come up sometime and see me?" were the scripted words for Mae West's invitation.)

"A rose is a rose is a rose." (No, Gertrude Stein did not write those words; what she did write was "Rose is a rose is a rose is a rose," with no starting *A* and with four uses of *rose.*)

"Music has charms to soothe a savage beast." (Perhaps euphemism is responsible for changing the line from the dramatist William Congreve; his words were "Music has charms to soothe a savage breast.")

"The huddled masses yearning to be free." (These words are not part of the Statue of Liberty's inscription; Emma Lazarus wrote: "Give me your tired, your poor, / Your huddled masses yearning to breathe free.")

27

COINAGES

STRETCHING THE LANGUAGE

AT DISNEYLAND, a salute to creativity includes a quotation from Thomas Edison: "The three great essentials to achieve anything worthwhile are, first, hard work; second, stick-to-it-iveness; third, common sense." *Stick-to-it-iveness* is a coinage, a phrase turned into a noun meaning "steadfastness" or even "one-track-mindedness" (another coinage).

"To coin a term" ranks among the most frequent clichés of public speaking. It dates back more than a century, rivaling the overuse of *proverbial*. Most of the time, though, the phrase is used with a term already coined, and the speaker is sarcastic enough to make that irony clear. When a legitimate term is being coined, the coiner may find a better way (such as "what I like to call") to point to its creation.

Words come into the language constantly. Some are nonce words, coined for a single occasion and never used again; others gain currency through frequent repetition in a wide variety of situations. The language already contains hundreds of thousands of words, and there may well be a specific word for even the most infrequent occasion (a one hundred fiftieth anniversary, for example, is a *sesquicentennial*).

When a situation requires a specific coinage, however, the

writer or speaker should be playful enough with the language to come up with a term. Paul Dickson's *Family Words* has a good example. A collective term, similar to *siblings* for brothers and sisters, was needed for nieces and nephews, and one family came up with *niblings.*

Playing with language spurs creativity. Functional shift, onomatopoeia, blends — many forms of new words are available. Before making up a word, however, a coiner should have some knowledge of how words are invented. Even though most users of English lack a thorough knowledge of classical languages (even Shakespeare was accused of knowing "small Latin and less Greek"), other ways of forming words are available to writers and speakers.

SHIFT FUNCTIONS DELIBERATELY

The trend may have started when the noun *contact* became a verb.

Also known as class cleavage, functional shift takes a word that fits one part of speech and transfers it to another, usually twisting nouns into verbs. "Bottom-line it for me," says a customer, transforming the noun phrase *bottom line* into a verb. A food server on a television talk show encapsulates her work with the statement "I waitress," and many train conductors now announce where the cars will "platform."

Perhaps the strongest form of functional shift comes from turning nouns into modifiers; called attributive nouns, these words work like adjectives. "Monster patrol" for babysitting, "Killer Cornbread" as a recipe, even "power language" — each uses a forceful noun to strengthen the word that follows. The practice is not so new as its users think. In a remark attributed to Daniel Webster, who died in 1852, the *monster* shifted: "Men hang out their signs indicative of their respective trades: shoemakers hang out a gigantic shoe; jewelers, a monster watch."

Using too much functional shift, however, sounds artificial

and makes the words seem affected or pretentious. Purists still resist the urge to convert *impact* into a verb or to use backformation to transform the noun *enthusiasm* into *enthuse,* although *enthuse* has now been in use for almost two centuries. Functional shift (or any new coinage, for that matter) will be most effective used amid a steady stream of Standard English. The writer or speaker thereby signals that the new usage is conscious, not a lack of word awareness.

Shakespeare was perhaps the most playful of all English writers, coining and shifting functions at will, even with proper names. Hamlet tells his players not to overplay their roles; the result of overacting, he says, is that "it out-Herods Herod."

COIN CAUTIOUSLY

The studio audience begins to laugh at pictures of Oprah Winfrey's old hairstyles, and Oprah encourages the response. "I am," she says, "uninsultable." Tom Shales, the television critic for the *Washington Post,* marvels at just how bad the performers on a variety show can be: "Singers who can't sing! Dancers who can't dance! Comedians who can't comede!"

From *uninsultable* to *comede,* various types of word formations prove useful to the writer or speaker searching for the right term. Lewis Carroll was fond of portmanteau words, also known as blends, which pull together two terms into one (named for the two-part traveling case). *Brunch* mixes "breakfast" and "lunch"; *smog* combines "smoke" and "fog." More recent blends include *telectorate* (television electorate) and *camcorder* (camera/recorder). These terms, too, can quickly be overdone, and objections are already being raised to *infomercial* and similar commercial blends.

Onomatopoeia is also a significant form of making words. This long term from Greek indicates words that imitate or echo sounds. The *chirp* of birds and the *hiss* of snakes or steam are examples of onomatopoeia, and even the technical revolution has witnessed an occasional coining, such as *zap* (from the supposed sound of a ray gun).

Sometimes a new invention comes from shortening an old word. This form, known as clipping, led to *memo* from "memorandum"; more recently, "maximum" has been clipped to *max* and "reputation" to *rep*. Sometimes a combining form is added: "commitment-phobic" describes somebody unable to enter a relationship. Adding *no* to a subject or a verb also produces a modern modifier: Jell-O's "No-Bake Pie," the "no-frills flight," a "no-kill animal sanctuary."

Knowing the audience can be helpful in determining how welcome a series of created words will be. Used with caution, coinages may be useful to language. Used with abandon, the same terms prove deadly.

UPDATE LANGUAGE AS NEEDED

The rare use of coinages comes into wordplay when the writer or speaker finds a lapse in the language. Often, though, the new term is unnecessary, and an expanded vocabulary may well provide the necessary term.

In an era of political correctness, the writer or speaker must be careful not to offend the audience. Some of the more conspicuous creations of this newspeak, though, will take time to gain validity. A waiter or waitress may prefer not to be called the gender-neutral *waitron*, while *mailman* has logically given way to *letter carrier*.

Recently, English has developed a new category of terms: retronyms. According to William Safire in a 1980 language column, the word was coined by Frank Mankiewicz, then president of National Public Radio, to label nouns forced to accept an adjective to stay current. Watch what happened to *watch*; once this timepiece became available in digital form, the old word became the retronym *analog watch.* The simple *guitar* that has no electric cord is now known as an *acoustic guitar.* Following are a dozen current retronyms, each followed by the reason for the updating:

1. oven: conventional oven (microwave oven)
2. gas: leaded gas (unleaded gas)
3. television: broadcast television (cable television)
4. game: day game (night baseball)
5. coffee: caffeinated or regular coffee (decaf)
6. mail: paper mail (electronic mail or e-mail)
7. year: calendar year (fiscal year or school year)
8. tea: hot tea (iced tea)
9. phone: rotary telephone (push-button phone)
10. walk-in theater (drive-in theater)
11. diaper: cloth diaper (disposable plastic diaper)
12. performance: live performance (taped performance or recording)

Beware adding too many adjectives, however; viewers of a television comedy series may well have pondered the alternative when told that "*Cheers* was filmed before a live audience."

Sometimes the best new word is an old one. Used in rare circumstances, an obsolete or obsolescent term may shade the meaning in a memorable way. Toni Morrison used *Beloved* for the title of a compelling novel, just as Eugene O'Neill named his final play with an archaic verb form: *The Iceman Cometh.*

The olden verb can help turn a well-worn phrase into a new expression. "The Lord loveth a cheerful giver," begins the notice on a church sign, adding, "He also accepteth from a grouch."

With the rarely used *score,* Abraham Lincoln added an archaic charm to the beginning of the Gettysburg Address, rendering "eighty-seven" as "Four score and seven years ago." His audience embraced the old term; today's listeners rarely welcome a speech that starts with a math problem.

In the examples that follow, coinages have been inserted. After each creation is an explanation of the word's formation. Many new terms will deservedly fail as awkward or heavy handed coinages. Whether the coinage will last or fade, though, has yet to be seen.

COIN COLLECTING

"Good Eats!" (This diner sign turns the verb *eat* into a noun by functional shift.)

"I've asked him to addition the figures and report the sum." (The noun *addition* has been turned into a verb.)

"Caution — Hazmat Trucks Use Right Lane." (This road sign uses an acronym formed from the first syllables of "hazardous material.")

"Home-Fashioned Candies." (The hyphenated "home-fashioned" is a blend of "old-fashioned" and "homemade.")

"We're helping babies transition to life outside the hospital." (Another functional shift, *transition* is a noun being tried as a verb.)

"This is what we call our Imagineering Department." (A Disneyland promotion uses this blend of *imagination* and *engineering,* later joining *animation* and *electronics* into *animatronics.*)

"His partner is honchoing the logistics of his firm's move." (The Japanese noun *honcho* is made into a verb, so its present participle must be *honchoing.*)

"I will in-service the new workers next week." (The phrase *in service* has been shifted into a verb meaning "to train or teach.")

"Fast-track your business degree." (This advice from a business school turns the noun phrase *fast track* into a verb.)

"Background us on what we're talking about." (This awkward request from a news anchor to a correspondent uses the noun *background* as a verb.)

"Effective campaigns contributed to our best quarter yet for new customer adds." (Just as *addition* went from noun to verb, the verb *add* can turn into a noun, made plural as *adds*.)

"She PTA's." (Even an abbreviation can be shifted from the noun phrase it stands for — Parent-Teacher Association — into a verb for attending the meetings.)

"I know of one potentuality that you are not prepared for." (This blend combines two nouns — *potentiality* and *eventuality* — into a new noun.)

"I am not a sneaker-into." (A television comedy tried to twist the verb phrase *sneak into* into a hyphenated noun.)

"That practice allows a mistake to be prolongated." (Another blend, this verb lengthens *prolonged* by combining it with *elongated*.)

28

ENERGY

PEP TALK

WRITERS AND SPEAKERS, beware — some subjects will be dull no matter how the words are presented. Take the weather, for example. Russell Baker in the *New York Times* recounted the weather assignment of a newspaper reporter, John Carr, forty years ago. Faced with a fifth straight day of the same weather, he submitted this story in its entirety: "Every day we have some weather, and today was no exception."

Bursts of energy in the language can propel speaking or writing. "Speak softly," said Theodore Roosevelt, an early proponent of power language, "and carry a big stick."

The big stick should be discouraged, but other techniques may be applied to enhance the force of phrases. Several of these keys give the speaker or writer an advantage that can build up meaning and tear down misunderstanding. Finding the right situations for each key is the goal of power language.

REVIEW THE OBVIOUS

Rarely does an audience's attention wander faster than when that audience is being told what is already known. Even in the most obvious material, something new or unfamiliar should be interspersed with the familiar. A failure to provide that something extra will result in an immediate power loss.

The key to this key is the double sense of *review:* "to see again" and "to make changes." Look over a supposedly final effort, whenever possible, for potential revisions. Just as clichés need to be played with, obvious wording should be given an unexpected spin.

"Dog bites man" is not news, as old editors pointed out; the news would be "man bites dog," now a clear violation of animal rights. Crossword puzzles and mystery stories show writers at their craftiest, working in double senses to confound their fans, at least temporarily. Murder mysteries are especially good at covering up; in *The Murder of Roger Ackroyd,* for instance, Agatha Christie keeps the murderer in full view until revealing the identity in the final pages. Comedians also know how to twist the obvious for effect: "When I'm good, I'm very good," Mae West said, "but when I'm bad, I'm better." View the material, then review it, aiming to find what needs to be changed to make the material stronger. Deleting an obvious expression here or there will add force to the phrasing.

Use the obvious to undercut the obvious. The word user may point to what seems true and, after inserting the conjunction *but,* point out the real truth. A talk show host stops her audience's jeering at a panel of vain young men and says, "We like to blame these guys, but if we women didn't go for them, there'd be no problem."

The value of viewing the obvious from a certain slant should never be underestimated. Emily Dickinson's poems often describe a subject without revealing it by name. What she calls a "Narrow Fellow in the grass" that leaves observers "zero at the bone" is a snake. Her poem that begins "I like to see it lap the miles" refers indirectly to a train.

Mark Twain knew the same trick. In his *Pudd'nhead Wilson's Calendar* entry for April 1, he wrote: "This is the day upon which we are reminded of what we are on the other three hundred and sixty-four." The reference to April Fool's Day is indirect, but it conveys as much force as Shakespeare's more direct wording for Puck in *A Midsummer Night's Dream:* "Lord, what fools these mortals be!"

CREATE SUSPENSE

"You are so predictable."

"I always know exactly what you're going to say before you say it."

"There you go again, repeating yourself!"

Far from being offended, the receiver of these comments should consider them fair warnings about weak wording. Whether in writing or speaking, the risk in being predictable is the boredom that causes an audience to lose interest.

Suspending information can produce more interest in the audience. *Wait for it* is a British expression, similar to the American *get this.* It comes before a surprise or an unusual fact, something that keeps the audience in momentary suspense.

Shakespeare knew how to provide suspense and overcome the obvious; his stage directions for *The Winter's Tale* force one character to "exit, pursued by a bear." The modern equivalent is the shock effect; from Alfred Hitchcock's film *Psycho* to Shirley Jackson's short story *The Lottery,* the viewer or reader is led to expect one outcome and startled by another.

When the effect is not to shock or disturb, the unexpected has its own charm. In the musical *Gypsy,* Stephen Sondheim's advice to strippers — "You Gotta Have a Gimmick" — is also true for writers and speakers who want their work to stand out. When the comedian Paul Reiser published his book *Couplehood,* he began on page 145 — a gimmick, yes, but also a different way to catch the reader's eye. Similarly, those who curse with abandon cannot expect to surprise with strong language; as one woman asked a group of language experts, "If I were to use those words all the time, what would I say when I'm really mad?"

INSERT HUMOR WHEREVER USEFUL

- "My wife ran off with my best friend," a country song says, "and I sure do miss him."
- "Husband and dog missing," reads a large sign in California. "Reward for dog."
- "I'm married," a game show contestant told the host, pausing to add, "And so is my wife."

Humor works wonders with words. Even religion adds a light touch; a church advertises itself as "fit to be tithed."

Probably the strongest ingredient in any word formula, humor must also be considered the most dangerous. Starting a speech with a joke or using a lighthearted anecdote to begin an essay is a time-tried way to win an audience. The wrong joke or anecdote, however, may lose that audience just as quickly.

Checking with others beforehand may be the best guard against a private or limited sense of humor. A student essay about a drama class veered off into a personal joke about the teacher, who was not amused. The dark humor of "But what did you think of the play, Mrs. Lincoln?" almost never works to the user's advantage.

Consider the effects of the words before proceeding with any attempt at humor. Humor that is hurtful hurts the message. In the right place, however, a comic line can decrease tension and increase interest. "We got rid of the kids," a bumper sticker states. "The cat was allergic."

CONTRADICT FOR EFFECT

Some people like to argue. Say that the weather is pretty, and they will complain about a cool wind. Compliment somebody's work, and they may nitpick about a minor error.

Such people fail to grasp the power of contradiction. This word comes from "to speak against," and the most forceful contradiction occurs when disagreement is rare. When the prince in Shakespeare's *Much Ado About Nothing* notes the mirth of young Beatrice, he suggests that her mother must have been merry when she was born. "No, sure, my lord," she contradicts in a heartbreaking line, "my mother cried."

Not all contradiction requires *no* or other negative wording, however. Sometimes it can take the forceful form of an unexpected response. The force comes from negating the other person's expectations, and that contradiction may not even require an opposing speaker or writer. In *Song of Myself,* Walt Whitman celebrates the power of self-contradiction. "Do I contradict myself?" he asks, answering: "Very well then I contradict myself, / (I am large, I contain multitudes)."

Negating the expectations of others makes the response all the stronger. Watch for the chance to deny forcefully, and discover the force of contradiction diction.

COUNT ON COURTESY

Perhaps an old-fashioned concept these days, courtesy still has its place in power language. In debate, rudeness and monopolizing the discussion can be countered and quickly cut by the right choice of words.

A youth leader in San Francisco speaks out on the force of phrases and encourages politeness in his audience. "You have to realize the power," he tells them, "of *please, thank you,* and *excuse me."* These words show consideration for others and give extra power to the speaker. In fact, thanking somebody who has refused to offer help may throw off the person enough that the help is forthcoming.

Sometimes all that is needed is the simple expression "I hear you" or "I understand what you're saying." These terms reassure the person who is trying to communicate and help the message move.

EXERCISE SILENCE FREELY

Silence provides hoarsepower.

"Blessed is the man who, having nothing to say, abstains from giving us wordy evidence of the fact," George Eliot wrote in an 1879 novel. The idea is ancient, though, translated as a maxim of Publilius Syrus in the first century B.C.: "I have often regretted my speech, never my silence."

There is power in silence. It makes an audience pay closer attention. "Speak low, if you speak love," Shakespeare advises. Fewer words, elliptical meanings, short speeches — all can work together to make the speaker or writer more powerful. Campaigning politicians have long used the power of paraleipsis; this rhetorical term refers to the debating trick of saying by pretending not to say ("I won't mention my opponent's failure to report income"). Paraleipsis, however, is a false silence, because words are still used to fill space.

In ancient Greece, the orator Alcibiades was famous for pausing to find the right word, and no one dared interrupt the silence. Not every empty space needs to be filled with sound. In *Othello*, the destructive Iago remains mysterious to the end; his final words — "Demand me nothing; what you know, you know: / From this time forth I never will speak word" — are among his most disturbing.

Silence does speak for its user. The fragrance Exclamation advertises that it "lets you make a statement without saying a word." That silent statement can express anything from joy to contempt. In 1978, the "refusenik" Anatoly Shcharansky defied the Soviet court that sentenced him to a labor camp; his last words to his judges were telling: "To you I have nothing to say."

Martin Luther King, Jr., expressed the positive power of silence in his eloquent acceptance speech for the 1964 Nobel Prize. "Occasionally in life there are those moments of unutterable fulfillment which cannot be completely explained by those symbols called words," he said. "Their meanings can only be articulated by the inaudible language of the heart."

Watch words carefully, listening to how others speak and reading how others write. No single source of energy in language is stronger than experiencing what has worked for others and what has failed. Following are the failed expressions that every user of power language should consider terms to terminate.

POWER OUTAGES

"As I've always said" — If it has been said, why repeat it?

"Let me say this about that" — Ronald Reagan may have popularized this introduction, but the six words are pure filler, giving the speaker time to think of something else to say.

"To make a long story short" — This phrase never appears in time to live up to its promise.

"And now, without further ado" — Drop these words from public speaking; in fact, almost any use of *ado* is "a don't."

"One might say" — These words are a coward's way out; either say it or don't.

"And so on and so forth." — These six words prove that the user cannot think of another example.

"I can promise you" — Watch out for this type of offer, which makes no promise at all; insist on "I promise you," no *can* about it.

"To state the obvious" — This phrase already tells you to ignore what follows.

"Get it?" — This question never turns a bad story into a joke.

"I mean" — Similar to "What I meant to say," this expression usually begins a second failure to communicate.

"I'm speechless" — This expression is never true.

"In a manner of speaking" — Watch this phrase, which means "I don't mean what I say."

"It goes without saying" — This expression should go without saying.

"So to speak" — Watch out for this phrase, a weak apology for a bad pun.

"Take my word for it" — Hearing this expression gives reason enough to check.

"How shall I put this?" — If the word user does not know, the audience cannot help.

"To tell the truth" — Use this phrase and risk being questioned about the truth of what was said before.

"Really" — Like *actually,* this adverb offers no "real" meaning.

"Believe it or not" — Avoid the risk of the audience not believing.

"Maybe I should have said" — This qualification does not increase an audience's confidence in the user.

"Trust me" — These two words are rarely, if ever, to be trusted.

"What's the best way to say this?" — Only the word user can answer this question.

V

POWER FUTURE

LANGUAGE IN THE NEXT MILLENNIUM

Star Trek FANS know that words and wording change with the times. The first *Star Trek* series, in 1966, began with a mission "to boldly go where no man has gone before." (In those days, a split infinitive was considered daring.) A generation later, *Star Trek: The Next Generation* redesigned the mission "to boldly go where no one has gone before."

That shift, from *man* to *one,* signals the future of language in the next millennium, as words become more socially acute. Language has never been stagnant: *girl* once referred to a young person of either sex, and over the centuries its use has become restricted to young females. *Boy* has borne the stigma of a racial slur and then been adopted within Black English with the in-group acceptability of *homeboy* (just as the once-offensive *queer* has regained acceptance in homosexual parlance). The topic of *sex,* a Victorian taboo, is now discussed widely, although often under the guise of *gender.*

What the future will hold for language cannot be predicted with certainty. There are, however, two areas that hold power for language users — wording with compassion and wording for computers — and they will become most potent as English moves into the third millennium.

First comes the power of *political correctness*. The name itself intimidates some and angers others; the process lends itself to easy parody (those who invariably show up late for appointments are the "temporally impaired"), but the reality is that language, much like society, will give way to some change. A male equivalent for the First Lady will eventually be needed, and *Miss* now sounds obsolete for *Ms.*

Those who dislike political correctness may find themselves more open to considering some of these changes by adopting a different sense of p.c.: *polite correctness.* Aiming to be "politely correct" allows the language user to show thoughtfulness and sensitivity, qualities worth cultivating in life as well as language. A passion for compassion adds power to writing and speaking.

PROGRESS WITH LANGUAGE

"I'm an actor," announces Cybill Shepherd on her television comedy, renouncing the *-ess* suffix of the female *actress.* "Be a Boy Scout," a television newscaster suggests, asking viewers to help out during an emergency. He pauses and adds, "Or a Girl Scout — whatever the case may be."

When the Modern Language Association asks for contributions to its journal, the guidelines for writers include this suggestion: "The MLA urges its contributors to be sensitive to the social implications of language and to seek wording free of discriminatory overtones."

Unless the word user wishes to alienate the audience, he or she must become aware of socially offensive language and understand the effect of his or her words. *He or she* and *his or her,* for example, acknowledge that the audience may consist of both males and females; the day of "the male embraces the female" in language use has passed. Unless an audience is exclusively male or exclusively female, words should acknowledge both sexes. *He or she* sounds wordy, and *he/she* looks bureaucratic. Others have tried the plural pronouns *they* and *their* to refer illogically to a single person. Even worse is a slip into second-person pronouns; a restaurant restroom posted the disturbing notice that "Employees must wash your hands." Supreme Court justices have reached an elegant compromise by choosing to use *he* sometimes and *she* sometimes within its decisions.

Language change cannot be dictated, even though Ted Turner has ordered the replacement of *foreign* by *international* throughout his broadcast organization. The day has not yet arrived that new or invented words can be forced to replace sexist words. Attempts to reduce *he or she* to the coined *se,* and *him or her* to *herm,* have not gained widespread acceptance. Nonsexist coinages such as *waitron* (for a waiter or waitress) and *shero* (for a female version of the nonsexist *hero*) are probably too mechanical to be successful.

More successful have been "gender-neutral" terms, such as *firefighter* for "fireman" and *worker* for "workman." Often these alternatives are longer: *members of Congress* takes two syllables more than "congressmen," and *letter carrier* requires two words for the shorter "mailman." Accuracy, however, may supersede brevity as a language requirement. The word *chairman* is frequently shortened to *chair,* but that makes the person sound like a piece of furniture; *chairman* and *chairwoman* are more accurate and provide more information about the person than the unisex *chairperson.*

Similarly, letter writers have long been disturbed by the problem of salutations. "Dear Sir" fails to address many readers, and "Dear Sir or Madam" sounds weak. Future correspondents will find more power in addressing the person or the title directly. "Dear Office Manager" may be substituted or, if the individual is not endearing, "To the Office Manager" is salutation enough.

Some gender-specific terms produce powerful imagery. A homeland, for instance, may be either a *fatherland* or a *motherland,* the parental metaphor stronger than the neutral term. Other attempts to remove sexism from language may sound comical; the slang *hitman* gains no elegance as a *hitperson* and loses its deadliness as a *hitter.*

Common sense should guide the word user through the minefield of charged words. The word *crippled* sounds harsh and should be replaced, although even that term is still used by some charitable organizations. Others have abandoned *handicapped* in favor of *impaired* or the more positive *challenged.* Among those who have reached an advanced age, many prefer *senior citizens* to *elderly* (*geezer* is obviously pejorative).

Knowing the audience may help a speaker choose the proper word. Terms for the mentally ill, for example, range from the offensive to the clinical. Psychiatrists have questioned the place of such words as *mad* and *certifiable* in the general language, and those who suffer from mental illness (and their families and friends) take exception to many of the slang uses. As society grows more aware of the effects of these terms, usage may change.

Until it does, however, humor may be the best tool for handling charged words. A sexist sentiment may now be twisted into a political bumper sticker: "A woman's place is in the House — and the Senate." Jokes about the driving ability of "dumb blondes" may be reworked into slogans for sports events; a golf tournament advertises, "Watch out for women drivers! See them burn up the course."

Politely correct language seeks to use terms that will include listeners and readers, not exclude them; such language may change from one generation to another. The word *black,* for example, is now vying with *African-American* as the dominant usage (although the use of the hyphen is controversial); another alternative, *people of color,* has been reworked by the overweight into the phrase *people of size.* Whatever terms are chosen, however, the choice should be conscious, never automatic.

ADVANCE WITH TECHNOLOGY

Despite the personal need for politeness, English is becoming more and more impersonal. The language of the future will be transmitted fast and facelessly. The speed of the information superhighway will have no limit, and tomorrow's word users should begin today to learn the ways of the Internet.

The good news for the future is that today's travelers on the Internet are already aware of problems with cyberlanguage. A disclaimer on one file states, "This list is not guaranteed to be complete, accurate, useful, grammatically sound, or spelled correctly." With software programs to supplement the human checking of grammar and spelling, technical errors should become obsolete.

Following are a dozen don'ts for the word-conscious user of tomorrow's technology. Even the "clueless newbie" (any first-timer on the information superhighway) can gain power by avoiding these computer complications.

1. Don't flame. (*Flaming* and *flame wars* refer to verbal assaults in cyberspace, and personal attacks do not reflect well on the writer; remember that rudeness never promotes power.)
2. Don't invite flaming. (Knowing the rules of cyberspace conversations can prevent flaming; those who do not know the rules should take the time to learn them.)
3. Don't shout. (Words typed entirely in capital letters are the Internet's equivalent of shouting, as in "DO NOT SHOUT!")
4. Don't monopolize. (Conversations, even electronic ones, are the interplay of ideas from more than one source, and others' ideas should be encouraged.)
5. Don't distort. (In responding to another's ideas, use key

words or ideas of that person without distorting or misrepresenting them.)

6. Don't be verbose. (Logorrhea is a disease that afflicts many word users, even those on the Internet; shape the message to fit the argument, and remember that brevity counts.)

7. Don't generalize. (Nothing upsets the high-tech writer more than such words as *never, always,* and *only;* examples that disprove the generalization will often be found amid paragraphs of flaming.)

8. Don't misuse words. (One cyberspace writer comments that unclear writing needs to be made *ambiguous;* the right word is *unambiguous.*)

9. Don't emphasize too much. (Avoid capital letters for emphasis; many Internet users place asterisks around words to *add* stress.)

10. Don't underestimate the audience. (The Internet is global; assertions such as "the nation's first" or "the nation's biggest" may provoke the question "What nation?")

11. Don't misspell. (When the electronically printed word is the only means of communication, spelling counts all the more; as one unfortunate user comments, "I was confusled.")

12. Don't overuse punctuation!! (An exclamation point is rarely necessary; two in a row are never needed.)

Understanding the effect of words is important now and will become even more important in the future. Knowing which words to use and which to avoid shows a type of kindness that marks the writer or speaker as somebody to respect. Ignoring or insulting the audience, on the other hand, leads to a rapid decline in rapport.

The maturing of the computer age has created a growing interest in the written word. Power language comes with finding the right word, spelling it correctly, and using it in the right context. Anything less will disappoint the reader and lead to a net loss in communication. The errors that follow have all blocked progress on the information superhighway.

NET LOSSES

"Curcke if cibcerb." (This seemingly foreign message is a church listing that should read "Circle of concern"; touch-typing on the wrong keys may create a message that causes concern.)

"We have diary farming in the north." (This lesson in agriculture needs its letters in the proper order; transpose the vowels in *diary* for the correct *dairy*.)

"The world is linked together by electronic media." (Watch out for redundancy; *linked* needs no *together*.)

"This was written to answer the frequent questions regarding about Florida." (Use either *regarding* or *about*; using both will raise frequent questions.)

"It will confirm that you has been retained in your current job." (Confirm the proper verb for its subject; do not retain *you has* in place of the proper *you have*.)

"This is a fictious band." (Even at cyberspeed, full words are still necessary; *fictious* should be *fictitious*.)

"She wrote a series of mysery novels." (Every letter counts; add a *t* to solve the mystery of *mysery*.)

"There are also hints that others maybe involved." (Remember the proper cyberspacing; when it is part of the verb, *maybe* should be *may be*.)

"The mood is broked." (Fix the past participle whenever it is *broked*; the right word is *broken*.)

"Watch this story!." (One mark of end punctuation is enough; either the exclamation point or the period should be deleted.)

"She stops by to talk ocassionally." (Check a dictionary, even an electronic one, to be sure to double the right letter; *ocassionally* should be *occasionally*.)

"Are her and him still married?" (The Internet still requires good grammar; *her and him* are objects, not the subjects *she and he*.)

"The content is the users responsibility." (Nouns that show possession need apostrophes; for one user, the form is *user's,* and use *users'* for more than one.)

"The recipe needs another flavoring that is better then lime juice." (The recipe for good wording requires choosing the right word and then spelling it correctly; here *then* should be *than.*)

"He was in a car accidnet." (Again, watch the order of the letters, or it is possible to have an *accidnet* on the information superhighway.)

CONCLUSION

UNLOCKING POWER LANGUAGE

KNOWING THE KEYS to power language is not enough. The writer or speaker must choose to use those keys, unlocking stronger words and finding new energy in expressions.

Almost a century ago, Twain remarked the difference in words between the lightning and the lightning-bug. Sound bites have replaced formal phrasing, but the keys to forceful wording remain the same. Today's writers and speakers still need to exercise care in wording to reap the benefits of power language.

Three more keys unlock the deepest sources of power language. They are followed by a skeleton key that is especially potent, underlying every other key in this book. If all the other keys are lost or forgotten, these four offer enough force to make even the most hesitant word user into a powerhouse of prose.

RESPECT THE AUDIENCE

The word user who respects the audience will never try to cheat or mistreat readers or listeners.

On a Friday episode of a soap opera, a character learns that her mother has left town. With murder in her eyes, she vows, "I'll track her down if it's the last thing I ever do." It was, however, just a cheap effect to end that episode; by the next show, she is professing her undying love for her mother.

In a similar way, a talk show features a woman who is fighting with neighbors. The host introduces the family's grandmother with "You'll never believe which side she is on!" and the audience waits for her to take the neighbors' side. After a commercial break, though, the grandmother says she sides with her granddaughter. The host, to lure the viewers to stay through the commerical, tricked the audience.

Checking and rechecking words can show respect for the audience. Sue Townsend, the British novelist, stopped in the middle of a public reading when she came to a passage in her book about a character's abrupt awakening: "He came wide awake swearing," she read, then stopped and shook her head. "That's a misprint. He should have come awake *sweating,* not *swearing.*"

Less sensitive to words was the bureaucratic writer of a memo mailed to a man who had recently died. The memo explained that the man's benefits would be stopped "because we received notice that you passed away." The memo's writer, obviously eager to end on an upbeat note, added, "You may reapply if there is a change in your circumstances."

Proper treatment of the audience includes sharing emotion that is genuine. "No tears in the writer, no tears in the reader," Robert Frost wrote in a 1939 essay, adding, "No surprise for the writer, no surprise for the reader."

Caring about people as well as words is the key to this key. "Look, then, into thine heart and write!" Longfellow suggested, just as his contemporary, Edgar Allan Poe, recommended: "Always write first things uppermost in the heart." It is the lesson learned in *King Lear* to "speak what we feel, not what we ought to say."

When possible, the topic for writing or speaking should be

something that the word user enjoys. Assigned essays or business reports may not generate much heartfelt enthusiasm, but the writer must look for ways to overcome boredom. Not every speech or story can end with a powerful epiphany similar to the conversion of Scrooge in *A Christmas Carol*, but some personal enthusiasm will catch the audience's attention or at least show respect for the audience.

As part of that respect, the modest statement will outweigh the self-serving statement. "In my humble opinion" sounds forced and falsely modest, but genuine humility has its own power. Consider the words of Shakespeare's soothsayer in *Antony and Cleopatra*. Blessed with gifts beyond most humans, the soothsayer makes only a modest claim: "In nature's infinite book of secrecy, / A little I can read."

APPLY RULES OF GRAMMAR AND USAGE

Strong English comes from good English. Knowing the rules of grammar and usage helps the writer or speaker apply them properly. Those who struggle to gain glamour should know that *glamour* began as a Scottish pronunciation of *grammar.*

The rules are important, but sometimes power is added by rejecting a specific rule. In the nineteenth century, the abolitionist Sojourner Truth was a powerful speaker for women's rights, with "And ain't I a woman?" as her oft-repeated question. In James Joyce's novel *Ulysses*, Molly Bloom says, "My patience are exhausted." Disagreement of subject and verb makes clever if not classy clauses: "We was robbed!" exclaimed Joe Jacobs after a 1932 heavyweight bout was decided against his boxer, and the incorrect *was* made the words memorable. Similarly, a cigarette manufacturer was more successful by advertising, "Winston tastes good like a cigarette should," even though *as* was the right word to replace *like.*

Know the rules, but also know when and where to apply them, keeping in mind the key that follows.

BREAK ANY RULE IF MORE POWER RESULTS

The last rule is not the least, but this rule applies only to those who do not work for or with a language purist. Only the individual can decide when formal Standard English must be used. There are times that winning words may not follow the rules, and the word user must learn to tell those times.

When reminded of the rule that prepositions should not end sentences, Churchill reportedly replied, "This is the sort of pedantry up with which I will not put," mocking those who disapprove of a sentence ending in *put up with.*

To further support the breaking of rules, George Bernard Shaw favored the split infinitive. When an editor corrected him, the playwright wrote of his indignation to the publisher: "Every good literary craftsman splits his infinitives when the sense demands it. I call for the immediate dismissal of the pedant on your staff. It is of no consequence whether he decides to go quickly or to quickly go."

Timing counts in any decision by the writer or speaker. Choosing the right time to write or speak takes careful planning. In "Smackwater Jack," Carole King sings about bad timing, pointing out the futility of conversation with somebody who holds a shotgun. Know the right time to approach the audience, and the act of communicating becomes easier. Professional speakers may practice tongue twisters before making a speech; writers may want to warm up with a letter to a friend.

The sense of timing will let the word user know when a limit is being exceeded. "This book might easily have been twice as long as it is," states Rudolph von Abele in the introduction to a biography, "but the importance of its subject would not have stood the strain." Others can also help the word user to gauge the effect of timing. A composition teacher tells of a professor with a "red-line test" — the professor would mark every essay with a red line at the point he would stop reading if he were not being paid.

To become expert in timing, the writer or speaker must practice. Education helps, but so does experience with people. "Unlearn'd, he knew no schoolman's subtle art," wrote Alexander Pope in tribute to a writer with the common touch, concluding, "No language, but the language of the heart."

Read and listen as much as possible. Everybody has favorite images, and finding out what makes others happy or angry, sad or worried, will improve any writer or speaker. Henry James, for instance, had a favorite expression, and it was captured by another novelist, Edith Wharton: "'Summer afternoon' — 'summer afternoon,'" James told her. "To me those have always been the two most beautiful words in the English language."

One final key serves as a skeleton key, which supersedes all the others:

THINK BEFORE WRITING OR SPEAKING

"Think before thou speakest," Cervantes advised in *Don Quixote* four centuries ago, and the advice still holds true. Think of this key as the all-encompassing rule of words. Thought and thoughtfulness can move the word user from weak wording to forceful phrasing, from timid terms to strong language.

"Sticks and stones may break my bones," the schoolyard saying taunts, "but words can never hurt me." Contrary to that notion, though, words do carry a physical power. An insult may produce a more lasting impression than a push or a punch. Afternoon talk shows bear daily witness to the effects of verbal abuse, and the user of power language should always keep the impact of words in mind. A man dying of cancer is interviewed about how the disease has changed his life. "I am more mindful," he answers, "of how I speak and what I say."

Poets and orators know the physical impact of power language. More than a century ago, Emily Dickinson composed a letter about this power. "If I read a book and it makes my whole body so cold no fire can ever warm me," she wrote, "I know that is poetry. If I feel physically as if the top of my head were taken off, I know that is poetry. These are the only ways I know it. Is there any other way?"

When words move an audience or make a mark, the writer or speaker has succeeded. The force belongs to those who know its ways and practice with their prose. Through a lifetime of careful wording, in fact, any word user can experience the rewards of power language.

INDEX